ETHICS, ECONOMICS AND FREEDOM

To Theresa and Bob Healy.
I wish we could all be like them!

Ethics, Economics and Freedom

The failure of consequentialist social welfare theory

TIMOTHY P. ROTH
The University of Texas at El Paso, USA

Ashgate

Aldershot • Brookfield USA • Singapore • Sydney

Published by
Ashgate Publishing Ltd
Gower House
Croft Road
Aldershot
Hants GU11 3HR
England

Ashgate Publishing Company
Old Post Road
Brookfield
Vermont 05036
USA

Ashgate website: http://www.ashgate.com

British Library Cataloguing in Publication Data
Roth, Timothy P. (Timothy Peter), 1943 -
   Ethics, economics and freedom : the failure of
   consequentialist social welfare theory
   1. Public welfare 2. Social policy
   I. Title
   361.6'1

Library of Congress Catalog Card Number: 99-76351

ISBN 0 7546 1009 8

Printed in Great Britain by
Antony Rowe Ltd, Chippenham, Wiltshire

Contents

HV
31
. R68x
1999

Acknowledgements

My intellectual debt to Professor Eirik G. Furubotn is enormous. While he may not agree with all that I have written, this book reflects his influence.

I wish to thank Juanita (Nita) Morgan for her dedication, patience and effort. Her computer and editorial skills made my work easier.

1 The Theoretical Foundations of the New Social Welfare Theory

1.1 The Frictionless Neoclassical World

The new Social Welfare Theory (SWT) rests upon the foundation of received, neoclassical theory. As such, SWT incorporates without revision the body of behavioral and technological postulates which define the neoclassical decision environment:

- The individual consumer is an autonomous, atomistic, classically rational utility maximizer. His preferences are both exogenously determined and stable, and defined on objects of choice whose qualitative and other properties are known with certainty.
- The individual producer employs a single-equation production function which, *inter alia*, is taken to be the only efficient--or output maximizing--technical alternative available. Moreover, the technology summarized in the production function is exogenously determined and fixed.
- Exchange and property rights are assumed to be unattenuated; that is, the implicit assumption is that the duties correlative to these rights are respected. Significantly, unattenuated exchange and property rights are instrumental to the achievement of first-best Paretian optima.
- Given these assumptions, and given that all exchanges occur instantaneously, transaction costs are assumed to be zero. In short, the decision environment is 'frictionless'.
- Finally, the received neoclassical theory is both institutionless and intendedly value-free. *Inter alia,* despite the implicit emphasis on the instrumentality of rights--a moral concept--little attention is paid to the role in objective functions and constraints of ethical and other norms. Indeed, a literature has grown up which emphasizes the potentially efficiency-enhancing effects of corruption.

Oddly, while this characterization of consumers' and producers' decision environments has come under increasingly robust attack, little attention has focused on the implications for SWT. This is important for various reasons, not the least of which is that efficiency is the only evaluative standard for public policy to which SWT gives rise. Yet the efficacy of the efficiency standard hinges importantly upon the theoretical and empirical foundations of neoclassical consumption and production theory.

The points of departure of this book are that, first, attention must be paid to the theoretical and empirical problems which inhere in neoclassical consumption and production theory. Much attention is therefore paid to the empirical content of neoclassical theory's behavioral and technical postulates, and to the logical inconsistencies to which the assumptions give rise. Second, contrary to the received doctrine, the new SWT is not 'value-free'. It is, in fact, a hybrid moral theory incorporating elements of goal- and rights-based moral theories.

1.2 The Treatment of Values and Institutions

The fact that it is intendedly value-free notwithstanding, SWT is typically expressed in preference-utilitarian terms. The focus is upon outcomes rather than upon decision procedures, with emphasis placed on the constrained maximization of social welfare. It follows, *pari passu*, that SWT incorporates elements of consequentialist, goal-based moral theories. At the same time, unfettered exchange and property rights are instrumentally important to the achievement of first-best Paretian optima. It follows that SWT incorporates elements of rights-based moral theories. SWT may therefore be understood to be a 'hybrid' moral theory.

This understanding runs counter to the received view that SWT--and its neoclassical wellspring--are a part of the corpus of 'positive' science. While much has been written about this, the essential point is that logical positivism is the methodological approach of choice for neoclassical and, *mutatis mutandis*, for social welfare theorists. Characteristically, emphasis is placed upon the scrupulous avoidance of explicitly normative statements, upon the permissibility--indeed, the desirability--of the employment of unrealistic generative assumptions, and upon the characterization of institutionless decision environments. That objective functions and constraints should neither affect, nor be affected by, formal or informal institutions is itself a reflection of the logical positivist methodology. On the one hand, while 'frictionless' transactions frequently have no empirical counterpart, an explicit accounting of institutional and other detail is, for the logical positivist, neither necessary nor sufficient for the generation of testable hypotheses. On the other hand, attention to institutional 'detail' would, inevitably, force attention upon both formal and informal institutions--presumably including ethical norms. This, of course, is inconsistent with 'positive' economic analysis. It is not surprising, therefore, that the frictionless transactions contemplated by neoclassical theory --and, *pari passu*, by SWT--occur in an institutional vacuum.

1.3 Social Welfare Theory and the Efficiency Standard

As has been emphasized, efficiency is the only evaluative standard for public policy to which SWT gives rise. Consistent with the intendedly value-free nature of SWT, the efficiency standard is itself characterized as 'value-free'. Given that SWT is, in fact, a hybrid moral theory, the efficiency standard must itself be value-loaded. Yet, even if we were to accept the claim that 'efficiency' has no normative content, social welfare theorists confront an anomalous situation: Proponents of the--presumably value-free--efficiency standard are occasionally inclined to argue that corruption may be efficiency-enhancing. This, in turn, has implications both for the internal consistency of SWT and for the efficacy of the efficiency standard as a tool of public policy evaluation.

1.4 Overview and Plan of the Book

Chapters 2 and 3 focus on the logical, empirical and other problems which characterize the theoretical foundations of SWT. The problems implicate both the Efficiency or Welfare Frontier [Chapter 4] and the Social Welfare Function [Chapter 6]. Difficulties arise when account is taken of some fundamental features of observable reality: Decision makers are boundedly rational, information asymmetries are ubiquitous, and opportunistic behavior is observable. In such an environment, there is no one-to-one correspondence between objective and subjectively perceived decision environments--especially when account is taken of the juxtaposition of the growth of knowledge and decision makers' cognitive limitations. It follows that transaction costs are positive, and the role of ethical norms, *inter alia*, in minimizing such costs becomes apparent. It is shown that, once account is taken of these phenomena, the space in which the Efficiency Frontier might be defined is indeterminate [Chapter 4].

Given the indeterminacy of the Efficiency Frontier, the only standard for public policy evaluation which is adduced from SWT--the efficiency standard --is called into question. Emphasis is placed on the fact that, contrary to the conventional view, the efficiency standard is not 'value-free'. More important, it is shown that, once the logic of the Efficiency Frontier is called into question, the welfare conditions typically employed to determine whether states-of-affairs are 'efficient' cannot meaningfully be employed.[1] This, in turn, calls into question the efficacy of market 'interventions' motivated by 'efficiency' [Chapters 4, 7 and 8].

Attention centers in Chapter 5 on the irreconcilability of consequentialist, utilitarian SWT and the moral force of rights. It is shown that social welfare theorists cannot regard instrumentally important--and therefore sanctioned--rights and correlative duties as having moral force. The essential point is that rights and correlative duties--in particular, the duty not to violate others' exchange and property rights--can always be overcome by purely utilitarian considerations. This, in turn, militates against the achievement of first-best Paretian optima. Equally important, it is shown that those economists--including social welfare theorists--who regard 'freedom' as intrinsically valuable (as morally exigent in itself), must recognize that utilitarian considerations: (a) can be used to rationalize the attenuation of rights, and (b) cannot be used in 'inverse form' to derive the rights which are regarded as instrumentally and/or intrinsically valuable.[2]

Chapter 6 addresses the implications for the Social Welfare Function of the juxtaposition of particular rights construals and 'meddlesome' preferences. It is shown that, when allowance is made for meddlesome preferences and rights *are* respected, Pareto optimal solutions may not be possible. In effect, the impossibility of what has been styled the Paretian liberal militates against the accommodation by SWT of minimal 'privacy' rights. This, along with the well-known difficulties associated with interpersonal utility comparisons (IUCs), calls into question the logical foundations of the Social Welfare Function.[3] Indeed, it is shown that it is possible, following Professor Buchanan, to question the notion of 'social preference'. Chapter 6 concludes with a discussion of the implications of the indeterminancy of the Social Welfare Function for consequence-based public policy evaluation. Emphasis is placed on the need to focus less on 'good' outcomes and more on 'right' institutions. With this in mind, Chapter 7 turns to a consideration of alternatives to consequentialist SWT.

While SWT is consequence-based and procedurally-detached, Amartya Sen proffers an alternative which is intended both to enrich the informational base of SWT and to introduce procedural considerations. Sen's approach is animated, in part, by recognition that Arrow's impossibility result raises profound difficulties for preference aggregation in the context both of aggregative social welfare judgements and in the case of social decision mechanisms. Equally important, Sen argues that normative social policy cannot be based only on preferences. Finally, it is Sen's view that, whereas consequences cannot adequately be appraised without any notion of the process which brought about the end-states, neither can procedures be judged without taking account of the attendant consequences.

For its part, the contractarian alternative to SWT takes as its point of departure observable features of reality including, *inter alia*, bounded rationality, information asymmetries, opportunistic behavior, path dependencies, and positive transaction costs. The complexity of this decision environment militates against the employment of consequentialist analysis. *Inter alia*, the unidentified nature of decision makers' preference structures means that, as Professor Buchanan has emphasized, 'There is no criterion through which [public] policy may be directly evaluated' (Buchanan, 1987, p. 247). On this logic, the focus of contractarian attention is not end-states or outcome patterns. Rather, evaluative attention centers on decision procedures, and on the formal and informal institutional regimes which both constrain, and are affected by, revealed choice behavior. Given its focus on decision procedures and the ethical and other 'rules of the game', the contractarian approach is accommodative both of the moral force of rights and their correlative duties, and of other moral dimensions of institutional evaluation. Of particular interest are institutions which: (a) acknowledge the lexical priority of rights and, therefore, of freedom; (b) maximize ethical behavior (and, thereby, reduce transaction and other costs); (c) are consonant with justice (in the sense of impartiality), and (d) minimize the deleterious effects of a growing competence-difficulty gap.[4] In short, the contractarian approach concentrates less on prediction and on 'getting the prices right', and more on 'getting the institutions right' (Williamson, 1994, p. 321). It is in this sense that the contractarian approach has much in common with what has come to be called the New Institutional Economics.

The point of departure of the final chapter is that the inertial intellectual force of the new Social Welfare Theory has imposed non-trivial costs. At the most fundamental level, it is clear that economists' reliance on SWT has resulted in the emergence of a theoretical and an empirical lacuna. It is, after all, tautological that institutionless, intendedly value-free analysis militates against the evaluation of alternative institutional regimes and, in general, inhibits the explicit invocation of the various dimensions of moral appraisal. Equally significant, while social welfare theorists may or may not regard rights as morally exigent in themselves, it is indisputable that they--and economists generally--regard rights as instrumentally important. On this view, the path to first-best Paretian optima requires that exchange and property rights be unattenuated. Moreover, from the perspective of institutionless, frictionless SWT, the role of 'government' can, at best, be characterized as minimalist.

Yet, it is clear that the efficiency standard has been employed to rationalize all manner of 'market interventions'. As a result, the role of 'government' has grown, exchange and property rights have been attenuated and, *pari passu*, freedom has eroded. In effect, a theory--SWT--which regards individual choice, self-determination, agency and independence as, at minimum, instrumentally important, has underwritten the growth of government.

From this perspective, contractarian analysis may be regarded as a constraint on Leviathan. On the one hand, an explicit accounting of observable features of reality--of, *inter alia*, bounded rationality, information asymmetry, opportunism, and the propensity to obfuscate--leads to a rejection of the efficiency standard. On the other hand, an accounting of these 'frictions' forces attention upon the role and importance of institutional constraints on, *inter alia*, special interests and their politician-agents. Whereas SWT concentrates on the evaluation of outcomes, contractarian analysis envisions institutions as public goods and focuses on standards of institutional evaluation. Among these standards are the priority of rights, the transparency of decision processes, the dissemination of information, impartiality, and the minimization of transaction and other costs. If, to paraphrase Professor Williamson, we get the institutions right, the outcomes will take care of themselves (1994, p. 321).

Notes

1   The point at issue goes beyond the well-known 'nirvana fallacy'. The fallacy obtains when the Efficiency Frontier is held up as a benchmark without taking explicit account of one or more real and unavoidable constraints. The point here is that the Efficiency Frontier cannot meaningfully be defined.

2   These considerations have basic relevance to SWT both because they call into question the logic of the path to first-best Paretian optima, and because the rights which can be overcome determine the distribution of freedom.

3   It is shown, moreover, that the IUC problem is manifestly more difficult if allowance is made for metapreferences, or preferences for preferences, and for path-dependencies. An implication of the former is that efforts may be undertaken to alter others' preferences. An implication of the latter is that learning, habit formation, the appearance of new objects of choice, and other phenomena may cause preferences to change. In either case, an IUC problem emerges for the same individual.

4   The essential idea is that the juxtaposition of the growth of knowledge and the increasing complexity of interactions against decision makers' limited cognitive abilities results in a growing disparity between objective and subjectively perceived decision environments. The resulting 'competence-difficulty gap' is congenial to the emergence of (sometimes contrived) information asymmetries and, *pari passu*, to opportunistic behavior.

2 The Neoclassical Behavioral Postulates: A Critical Appraisal

2.1 *Homo Economicus*

There is little question that the elegance, comparative simplicity and apparent generality of neoclassical theory is compelling. Central to the paradigm is *homo economicus*. This classically rational decision maker does not simply have consistently ordered and stable preferences.[1] He affects narrowly self-interested, utility maximizing decisions in a frictionless world characterized by zero transaction costs and unambiguously defined and unattenuated property rights. It is this institutionless, intendedly value-free decision environment upon which is built the received, ordinal utility theory and, *mutatis mutandis*, the new SWT.

The commitment to this paradigm is manifested by its proponents' insistence that, with minor adaptation, virtually all observed human behavior can be predicted and, or, explained.[2] Interestingly, the general thrust of this argument has gained some currency among other social scientists. This has occurred at the same time that New Institutional, experimental and other economists have become increasingly skeptical about the behavioral postulates which characterize the received theory.[3]

As is well known, *homo economicus* is an atomistic, autonomous decision maker who maximizes a well-behaved objective function subject to one or more exogenously imposed constraints. The central property of the objective function is captured by classical rationality, while the latter include intertemporally stable, exogenously determined tastes and preferences. The constraints are, typically, assumed to be beyond analysis while, in contemporary usage classical rationality has been taken to mean that economic man acts purposefully and in his narrow self-interest (Persky, 1995, p. 223).[4] For their part, the objects of choice are generally taken to be purchasable economic goods whose physical and technical characteristics are known with certainty, and whose associated property rights bundles are both well-defined and unattenuated. In this 'frictionless', institutionless environment, information asymmetries are absent, opportunistic behavior is not observed, and the vectors of goods' characteristics do not contemplate their ethical attributes. This, in turn, is consistent with the intendedly value-free focus of the analysis.

A corollary of all of this is that there is a one-to-one correspondence between economic man's objective and subjectively perceived decision environments. This is true, moreover, whether the desideratum is static- or multi-period utility maximization. *Inter alia*, stability of preferences assures that evolutionary phenomena--including learning, the appearance of new economic goods, or the discovery of extant but heretofore unaccounted for options--are either ruled out, or that these and other path-dependent phenomena do not alter the underlying preference structure.

While little emphasis is placed upon it, the frictionless decision environment contemplates a peculiar neoclassical 'contract'. In the situation envisioned, classically rational, fully-informed decision makers engage in instantaneous exchange. Immunized from the effects of information asymmetries, and assured that their exchange and property rights are not--and never will be--attenuated, opportunistic behavior is not at issue. In the event, transaction costs and, *pari passu*, the *ex ante* and *ex post* costs of contract enforcement are zero. Imperfect or relational contracting is, perforce, nonexistent.

While various elements of this characterization of economic man have been subjected to increasingly robust attack both within and outside the economics profession, my interest centers, initially, on the classical rationality postulate.[5]

2.2 Some 'Frictions'

Classical rationality is a generative--as opposed to an auxiliary--assumption (Melitz, 1965, pp. 42-46). While generative assumptions constitute statements which serve to derive hypotheses, auxiliary assumptions consist in statements used in conjunction with the hypotheses to deduce predictions. From the positivist or instrumentalist methodological perspective, generative assumptions--and, therefore, classical rationality--need not be realistic.[6] On this interpretation, the test of a model is not the realism of generative assumptions. The appropriate test is the correspondence of predictions with observable reality.[7]

While the logic of the positive or instrumentalist position is unassailable,[8] there is a fundamental problem: The key auxiliary assumption--stability of tastes and preferences--cannot be tested independently of the classical rationality postulate.[9] It follows, *pari passu*, that tests of predictions are neither confirmatory nor disconfirmatory (Roth, 1998, Chapter 1, esp. pp. 15-16).[10]

The literature typically characterizes this problem as reflecting the presence of an unidentified exogenous variable; the consumer's tastes and preferences (Roth, 1998, p. 9). This, however, is fundamentally misleading. The presumed exogeneity of preference structures either denies or ignores a panoply of evolutionary and other path-dependencies which appear to influence consumers' tastes and values.[11] It seems clear, for example, that learning and the emergence of new products affect preference structures. Indeed, sensitivity to the notion that learning may alter preference structures was one of the catalysts to the Stigler/Becker effort to show that addiction, habit formation and other intertemporal phenomena are consistent with the stability of 'underlying preferences' defined over 'fundamental aspects of life'. It is clear, however, that these presumably stable 'metapreferences' can only be inferred; they do not govern choices among purchasable economic goods.[12] In effect, the Stigler/Becker approach invokes 'fixed but invisible preferences' which '. . . are operationally indistinguishable from values mutable with respect to any observable behavior and subject to evolution in response to time and experience' (Aaron, 1994, p. 6). The essential difficulty is that virtually any observed behavior can be ascribed to 'underlying preferences'. It follows, *pari passu*, that models employing this approach are not disconfirmable

> . . . it is not clear what set of observations would cause economists to abandon . . . the version [of the neoclassical theory of consumer behavior] which assumes that preferences . . . are exogenous and identical over time and space. . . . (Pollak, 1985, pp. 584-585).

There is, moreover, a growing body of evidence that evolutionary phenomena do affect preference structures.[13] The large and growing literature on anomalous behavior[14]--behavior judged to be inconsistent with classical rationality and expected utility theory--may find its genesis in the apparently irremediable fact that preference structures are path-dependent; that they depend, *inter alia*, upon learning, experience and, perhaps, upon higher-order preferences (North, 1994). It is apparent, for example, that some persons have preferences for preferences, and that they seek to alter others' preferences (Buchanan, 1994b, pp. 74-77). Equally important, internal conflict may complicate decision processes.[15] The consumer may, for example, be tempted by the convenience of a handicapped parking space but, at the same time, be disinclined to prevent a handicapped person from using the allotted space. The same consumer may enjoy smoking but chooses not to do so in public because he has learned that secondary smoke may harm others. Given that such phenomena are implicated in the choice process, it is plausible to conclude that 'To assert that preferences are stable is . . . a palpable absurdity' (Aaron, 1994, p. 17).[16]

The endogeneity of preference structures is clearly irreconcilable with the orthodox conception of economic man.   Moreover, the endogeneity of preference structures strikes at the heart of positive or instrumentalist methodology: *Inter alia*, preference endogeneity means that predictive models whose agent is *homo economicus* can neither be confirmed nor disconfirmed. Finally, *homo economicus'* atomistic, autonomous decisions are difficult to reconcile with the intervention of ethical and other behavioral norms; norms which may properly be regarded as arguments of utility functions and/or as constraints on behavior

> I am now surprised, belatedly, that most efforts of economists, including my own, to derive a logic of personal rule following have 'jumped over' the rather elementary logic of moral constraints. . . . (Buchanan, 1994a, p. 133).[17]

If preference endogeneity, internal conflict and the intervention of ethical and other behavioral norms are phenomena of which account must be taken, the same must be said of cognitive limitations. As Professor Simon has emphasized, there is a discrepancy

> . . . between the perfect rationality that is assumed in classical and neoclassical economic theory and the reality of human behaviour as it is observed in economic life. The point [is] not that people are consciously and deliberately irrational . . . but that neither their knowledge nor their powers of calculation allow them to achieve the high level of optimal adaptation of means to ends that is posited in economics (Egide & Marris, 1992, p. 3).

In short, decision makers are boundedly rational (Conlisk, 1996). While there is no generally accepted definition of bounded rationality (Furubotn and Richter, 1997, p. 39), Simon's characterization of agents' decision environments comports with the notion of a competence-difficulty gap (C-D gap). Whereas neoclassical choice theory assumes 'that there is no gap between an agent's competence and the difficulty of the decision problem to be solved' (Heiner, 1983, p. 562), observed regularities in choice behavior

> . . . can be fruitfully understood as 'behavioral rules' that arise because of uncertainty in distinguishing preferred from less-preferred behavior (Heiner, 1983, p. 561).[18]

The essential point is that, for the boundedly rational decision maker, optimization is 'a special case occurring when uncertainty (the C-D gap) approaches zero' (Wilde, LeBaron and Israelsen, 1985, p. 403). Yet, the 'special case' is likely not to be observed because one of the implications of knowledge growth is that 'Each of us is today relatively far more ignorant than was a well-educated person at the dawn of the nineteenth century' (Wilde, LeBaron and Israelsen, 1985, p. 405). Add to this the increasing complexity of interpersonal relationships and it is clear that there is a growing gap between agents' competence and the difficulty of the decision problems confronting them. It follows, *mutatis mutandis*, that there is a growing gap between decision makers' objective and subjectively perceived decision environments.

That cognitive limitations constitute an endogenous constraint on choice is, it seems clear, a brute fact of life.[19] While cognitive limitations have many implications, among the most important is that information asymmetries are pervasive. It is clear, for example, that decision makers are characterized by differing stocks of knowledge, by differing abilities to process extant and incremental knowledge, and by an inability always to disentangle the effects of random events generated by the environment from those effects which obtain because of opportunistic behavior. An essential point is that, in the face of these 'frictions', principals enter into relational contracts with agents.[20] Given that performance and *quid pro quo* provisions cannot anticipate all eventualities, such contracts are necessarily incomplete. Yet the motivation behind such contracts is transparent: Principals seek to minimize the *ex ante* and *ex post* costs of monitoring their agents' behavior.

While much can be said about this, the irremediable fact is that, because random events affect observed results, '. . . the principal cannot conclude anything definite about the actions of the agent by merely considering the record of actual events' (Furubotn and Richter, 1991, p. 18). And it is precisely the confluence of cognitive limitations and random events which is congenial to the emergence of opportunistic behavior; to '. . . the incomplete or distorted disclosure of information, . . . to calculated efforts to mislead, distort, disguise, obfuscate, or otherwise confuse' (Williamson, 1985, p. 47). Given the 'frictions' which inhere in such a decision environment, allowance must be made for still another 'brute fact': In a world characterized by information asymmetries, random events and opportunistic behavior, 'completely accurate monitoring and full enforcement of property rights are impossible' (Furubotn, 1994, p. 25). Stated differently, in a world characterized by cognitive limitations and other 'frictions', the rights to use, to appropriate returns, and to change the form of assets may be systematically--and surreptitiously--attenuated.

If nothing else were said, it is clear that, once account is taken of cognitive limitations, of information asymmetries, and of opportunistic behavior, an economic case can be made for an explicit accounting of the role and importance of ethical norms.[21] In effect, the rarified decision environment of the atomistic, autonomous, narrowly self-interested and classically rational *homo economicus* must give way to one in which, *inter alia*, ethical norms appear both as arguments of utility functions and as endogenously determined constraints. It is, after all, tautological that the intervention of ethical norms militates against the emergence of opportunistic behavior. This, in turn, contributes to the minimization of transaction costs; in particular, the *ex ante* and *ex post* costs associated with relational contracting. Granting this, an *a priori* case can be made for what Professor Buchanan characterizes as "resource commitment to 'preaching'" (Buchanan, 1994a, p. 126). On this view, moral constraints play an instrumental role in the functioning of the marketplace:

> A market economy is perhaps best viewed as a network of rights and obligations based on contracts and legal requirements (Furubotn and Richter, 1997, p. 140).

Roughly paraphrased, respect for rights and correlative duties is not simply the *deus ex machina* by which transaction costs are minimized. Respect for rights and correlative duties and, *pari passu*, trust, are the essential lubricants of an increasingly impersonal market economy. Indeed, if one adopts the view that 'freedom' is morally exigent in itself, then respect for the rights which determine freedom's distribution is intrinsically valuable. On this account such values as honesty are, *mutatis mutandis*, intrinsically valuable. Equally important, it is clear that

> . . . the effectiveness of markets (in which people are free to pursue individual self-interest) depends on a political system that successfully constrains individuals from pursuing self-interest through political channels. . . .

> The very origins of successful markets are seen to be dependent on institutional constraints operating on political actors (Miller, 1997, p. 1198).[22]

While formal, constitutional constraints on political agents have a role to play, so too do informal institutional regimes, including ethical norms. Indeed, it is possible to construct constitutional, legislative and other formal institutions in a manner which is consonant with standards of moral evaluation. This is the subject matter of Chapter 8.

It is clear that the functioning of markets depends importantly on the intervention of ethical constraints. It is also clear that economists have paid little attention to the notion of value formation through public discourse. This, it seems, is a reflection both of the intendedly value-free nature of neoclassical theory, and of the propensity of economists to regard preferences and values (or moral tastes) as exogenously determined. Indeed, whereas sociologists regard preferences and values as 'results of enduring exchanges and social contracts' (Baron and Hannan, 1994, p. 1117), the inclination of economists is, by and large, to adopt the convention employed by Kenneth Arrow (1951, p. 7) '. . . we will . . . assume . . . that individual values are taken as data and are not capable of being altered by the decision process itself'.

While Professor Arrow's motivation was to simplify the analysis of the methods of social choice, he acknowledges that 'the unreality of this assumption has been asserted by such writers as Veblen, Professor J.M. Clark, and Knight' (1951, p. 8). To that list could be added, among others, Adam Smith (1759), John Stuart Mill, Amartya Sen and, as has been emphasized, James Buchanan. The essential point is that, '. . . the practical reach of social choice theory . . . is considerably reduced by its tendency to ignore value formation through social interactions' (Sen, 1995, p. 18).

Granting the logic of what has been said, intendedly value-free neoclassical choice theory must give way to a theory which acknowledges both the endogeneity of preference and value structures, and the efficacy of 'preaching' or 'investing in ethical persuasion' (Buchanan, 1994b, p. 62). More broadly,

> The methodological individualist must . . . acknowledge the relationships between individual utility functions and the socioeconomic-legal-political-cultural setting within which evaluations are made (Buchanan, 1991, p. 186).

In effect, economic theory must acknowledge both the reciprocal nature of preference and value structures and the 'socioeconomic-legal-political-cultural setting', and the role and importance of ethical norms in the functioning of markets. It is, after all, tautological that ethical norms have a role to play in minimizing the deleterious effects of opportunistic behavior.[23] The difficulty is that intendedly value-free and institutionless neoclassical theory does not contemplate a world in which 'The morality of economic agents influences their behavior and hence influences economic outcomes' (Hausman and McPherson, 1993, p. 673).

That said, the question becomes, How might values--in the sense of ethical norms and moral tastes--be incorporated in the analysis of agents' decision processes?

While they may be regarded as preliminary, empirical findings in evolutionary and other branches of psychology may be helpful. There is evidence, for example, that

> One or more of [a] collection of distinct [cognitive] processing units weighs or tries to weigh economic goods according to the logical laws of transitivity, but other processors register utility in at least five other ways (Aaron, 1994, p. 15).

On this interpretation, utility derives from the consumption of goods and services. But it also derives from self-reference, from helping (hurting) others, from caring about others as 'ends', from interpersonal relationships, and from setting goals and achieving them.[24]

It is apparent that these distinct utility domains do not comport with the decision environment contemplated by *homo economicus*. *Inter alia*, utility domains cannot be captured by a single-equation, intertemporally stable and exogenously determined utility function. They may, however, be represented by multi-equation preference and value systems; by multi-equation utility functions defined for the same individual.[25] A defining characteristic of such systems is their ability to represent what Aaron has called 'the most palpable reality of all our lives--internal conflict' (Aaron, 1994, p. 15). Appeal to a multi-equation utility function facilitates the formal modelling of such internal conflicts as those concerning whether or not to park illegally, to smoke, or to purchase a good which, it is suspected, has been stolen. It follows that formal modelling can contemplate the ethical attributes of goods and, in general, can attend to the question of whether an activity 'should' or 'should not' be under-taken. If one grants that the 'frictionless' world contemplated by neoclassical theory has no operational counterpart, this is self-evidently important.

While the technical difficulties associated with multi-equation utility systems are manifest, they are not insurmountable.[26] And, while it could be argued that the approach might, at best, enable economists to rationalize behavior *ex post*, that may be the price which has to be paid (Aaron, 1994, p. 17). The logic of methodological pluralism argues that prediction and expla-nation are, after all, not the only legitimate goals of science (McCloskey, 1983). Moreover, as has been emphasized, there are profound methodological problems associated with the empirical confirmability (disconfirmability) of models which assume classical rationality and stability of preferences. Finally, as Sen has emphasized

> There is a lot to be done. . . . Quite a lot of high-brow economics . . . accepts the appropriateness of the standard general equilibrium model, with everyone

pursuing their self-interest, given tastes and technology. . . . But the high ground is not secure at all. The most basic element of such modelling, namely the motivation of human beings, is not well addressed (Klamer, 1989, p. 147).

Plainly, the 'high ground' is not secure. In part, this is a corollary of neo-classical economists' intellectual commitment to positive, intendedly value-free, institutionless analysis

. . . [the blame] must be laid squarely on the shoulders of the economists, who have separated economics from its initial moorings as a part of moral philosophy . . . . orthodox economic analysis has no place for recognizing much of the ethical interdependence among participants in an economic nexus. . . . (Buchanan, 1994b, pp. 82-83).

More broadly, the 'high ground' is not secure because neoclassical theory takes no account of the 'frictions' which actually characterize agents' decision environments. Unfortunately, when account is taken of these 'frictions' the 'high ground'--in the sense of the new SWT--is unattainable. As we shall see in Chapters 4 and 6, an explicit accounting of bounded rationality, information asymmetries, opportunism, positive transaction and decision costs, and the intervention of moral evaluative standards renders both the Efficiency Frontier and the Social Welfare Function indeterminate. For the moment, however, my interest centers on the other foundation upon which SWT's 'high ground' is built. In Chapter 3, I turn to a critical appraisal of the neoclassical understanding of 'technology'.

Notes

1   For a discussion of the definitions of rationality encountered in the literature, see Klamer, 1989. See also Roth, 1998.

2   'Adaptation' is typically accomplished by the simple expedient of introducing different arguments into decision- makers' objective functions and, or, the addition of 'appropriate' constraints.

3   See Furubotn, 1994; Williamson, 1993, and Conlisk, 1996.

4   The notion that individuals act in their narrow self-interest is sometimes used to rationalize patently unethical behavior. See Cheung, 1996; Lui, 1996, and Tullock, 1996.

5   For representative critiques of economic man, see Cox and Epstein, 1989; Elster, 1989; Furubotn, 1994; Nelson, 1995; North, 1994; Sen, 1995; Tversky and Thaler, 1990.

6   For a discussion of the conditions which must be satisfied if an assumption is to be 'realistic', see Wong, 1973, p. 317.

7   See Roth, 1998. See also Keita, 1992.

8   See, for example, Boland, 1981.

9   See Robinson, 1962.

10   See also Robinson, 1962, p. 50.

11   'Values' may be understood to be moral tastes. See Buchanan, 1994a; Sen, 1995. See Buchanan, 1994b, pp. 76-77 on the mutability of preferences.

12   For a critique of the Stigler/Becker approach, see Aaron, 1994, p. 6; Furubotn, 1994; Roth, 1998. It is at least arguable that Professor Becker has begun to rethink his position. In his 1993 Nobel lecture, he observed that 'Actions are constrained by income, time, imperfect memory and calculating capacities, and other limited resources'. He concludes that 'My work may have sometimes assumed too much rationality' (Becker, 1993, p. 402).

13   See Aaron, 1994; Sen, 1995. See also Smith, 1994; Bowles and Gintis, 1993.

14   See, for example, Tversky and Thaler, 1990.

15   See Hausman and McPherson, 1993, p. 688.

16   See also Buchanan, 1994b, p. 76.

17   The essential point is that, 'Economics models persons as maximizers of utility, but arguments in utility functions include rules that restrict the choices that are made' (Buchanan, 1994a, p. 128). For an approach to including moral concerns in preferences and constraints, see Dowell, Goldfarb and Griffith, 1998.

18   As will be emphasized, these behavioral rules may include moral constraints. See, for example, Buchanan, 1994b, p. 65.

19   See Buchanan, 1994a.

20   See Furubotn and Richter, 1991.

21   See Buchanan, 1994a; Wilde, LeBaron and Israelsen, 1985; Hausman and McPherson, 1993, 1996.

22   See also Buchanan, 1994b, Chapter 3, esp. pp. 71, 73 and 80; Furubotn and Richter, 1997, pp. 417-420; Prybyla, 1995.

23   Indeed, the Nobel laureate econometrician, Trygve Haavelmo has come to the view that economics generally, and econometrics, in particular, must take account of the reciprocal relationship between 'economic results' and the 'structure of rules and regulations within which the members of society have to operate' (1997, p. 15).

24   Interestingly, this understanding of individuals' utility domains comports with Adam Smith's view of man. See, for example, Smith, 1759, Part I, Section I. See also Muller, 1993.

25   These ideas are more fully explored in Chapter 4, below.

26   See Furubotn, 1967; Roth, 1975.

3 The Neoclassical Approach to Technology: A Critical Appraisal

3.1 Introduction

If, to paraphrase Professor Sen, the high ground is not secure, it is not only because the motivation of decision makers is not well addressed. As we shall see, the technological foundations of SWT are encumbered by internal inconsistencies, by an artificial delimitation of the 'firm's' technical options, and by a failure to account for positive decision costs.

A defining characteristic of the neoclassical approach is the *a priori* specification of a single-equation production function, with no account taken of the choice of technique problem which is characteristic of observable reality. This, in turn, has implications for SWT; in particular, for the derivation of the production possibility frontier [PPF] and, *pari passu*, for the Efficiency Frontier. While these issues are more fully developed in Chapter 4, my interest centers here on a brief explication of the neoclassical technical environment, and of the logical and other problems associated with the theory.

At the heart of the neoclassical formulation is the presumption that production proceeds under the technical restrictions imposed by a single-equation, flow-flow production function,

$$q = f(x_1, x_2) \tag{3-1}$$

where q denotes output per unit time, and the service flows x_1 and x_2 denote, respectively, manhours and machinehours.

Inter alia, (3-1) is presumed to be the only 'efficient' or output maximizing technical alternative available. While little attention has centered on it, an implication of this assumption is that the firm does not confront a 'choice of technique' problem. Moreover, in its short-run configuration, (3-1) is presumed to reflect perfect adaptability. In effect, 'efficiency' requires that, as movement along the short-run expansion path [SREP] proceeds, the physical form of the capital stock which generates the 'fixed' service flow must be instantaneously and costlessly adapted to the changing rates of use of the 'variable' service flow:

Although no great emphasis is placed on the matter, it is implicit that the fixed agent has a unique and optimal physical form in each combination. This . . . suggests that the form of the fixed agent must always be changed, . . . and improved if movement is to be made from one operating point to another along the (classic) short-run expansion path (Furubotn, 1964, p. 22).[1]

It is tautological, therefore, that the theory implicitly acknowledges the existence of differentiated forms of capital input types. The situation may be understood by appeal to mnemonic notation: K_2 denotes the nonhuman or physical capital stock which generates the 'fixed' service flow, x^0_2. But, as movement along the SREP proceeds, alternative rates of use of the variable input, x_1, are employed. To each rate of use of x_1, x_{1j}, $j = 1,2, \ldots , $ n, there corresponds a unique, instantaneously and costlessly adapted K_{2j}. Each of the K_{2j}, $j = 1,2, \ldots , $ n may, given the structure of the model, be understood to possess a unique vector of physical characteristics. In effect, to each point on the SREP there corresponds a unique, differentiated form of the capital input type, K_2, K_{2j}.

Clearly, the perfect adaptability assumption is false *a priori*. Given that it is a generative assumption--and given that the purpose of the model is prediction--perfect adaptability is an admissible assumption. There is, however, an important proviso: If logical inconsistencies are to be avoided, the implications of such assumptions must be adduced.[2]

In the instant case, perfect adaptability implies the instantaneous and costless 'metamorphosis' of a capital input type. What seems not widely to be acknowledged is that, because each differentiate of the capital input type, K_2, possesses unique physical characteristics, the technical properties of the associated service flow are not invariant.[3] This is an elementary engineering phenomenon. Yet this brute fact gives rise to a logical conundrum: As adaptation proceeds--and, *pari passu*, as the technical properties of the 'fixed' service flow change--the production function changes. It follows, therefore, that movement along the neoclassical short-run expansion path is a logical impossibility (Roth, 1974).[4]

3.2 The Implications for the Contract Curve in Input Space

At one level the difficulties which attend the logic of the neoclassical SREP do not have basic relevance to SWT. It is after all clear that the logic of the contract curve in input space requires that, for all producers, all inputs be simultaneously variable. In effect, generation of the contract curve and, *pari passu*, the PPF, does not contemplate movement along neoclassical short-run expansion paths.

At another level, the perfect adaptability conundrum does have immediate relevance to SWT. The core problem is the irremediable fact that differentiated forms of distinct capital input types generate technologically distinguishable service flows. Yet, we know that, at a cross-section of time, capital input types--whether human or nonhuman--do occur in differentiated forms. This, in turn, has implications for the specification of the firm's technology.

Reduced to its essentials, fundamental engineering considerations militate against the specification of a single-equation, 'efficient' production function. Account must be taken of the fact that output of a product may be secured via the employment of alternative differentiates of capital input types. This is true of elementary production processes such as sawing wood.[5] But it is also true of such complex production processes as the provision of medical services. The technical environment envisioned may be summarized by appeal to a multi-equation stock-flow production function of the form[6]

$$q_t = g_i (x_{1jt}, x_{2kt} | K_{1j}, K_{2k}) \tag{3-2}$$

where $j = 1, 2, \ldots, p$
$k = 1, 2, \ldots, r$
$i = 1, 2, \ldots, s$
and $s = p \cdot r$

The logic of system (3-2) suggests that each of the s competing production subfunctions has as its parameters differentiates of the capital stocks, K_1 and K_2. Thus, production subfunction g_1 has as its parameters K_{11} and K_{21}. The physical and technical properties of K_{11} and K_{21}, in turn, determine the technical properties of the associated service flows, x_{11t} and x_{21t} employed per unit time, t.

Given this understanding of the technical environment, the producer is confronted with a 'choice of technique' problem: Given its desideratum, which of the s production subfunctions should the firm employ?

If the choice of technique problem is a definable feature of observable reality, so too are bounded rationality and positive transaction costs (Chapter 2). Yet, as Professor Furubotn has observed

. . . when entrepreneurs have limited cognitive ability and are forced to use time and other resources to acquire, retain and interpret complex information, the basic nature of the firm's problem is changed. By contrast with the orthodox case, knowledge is seriously incomplete--e.g., the firm can no longer begin its decision-making process with information on all of the technological options that are, in principle, knowable (mimeo, 1997, p. 16).

The fact that the firm's knowledge is 'seriously incomplete' is under-scored by the fact that, while system (3-2) is heuristic, it does not, in most cases of practical importance, exhaustively represent a producer's technical options. This is true since, *inter alia*, system (3-2) acknowledges only two capital input types. Presumptively, production processes typically contemplate the simultan-eous employment of more than two capital input types, with many of these appearing in differentiated forms. Granting this, were nothing else to be said, explicit acknowledgment of this phenomenon would serve to expand the definable array of production subfunctions--or 'techniques'--contemplated by system (3-2). Moreover, an exhaustive representation of the new, expanded system would presume exhaustive knowledge, at a cross-section of time, of the number and technical properties of each of the differentiates of each of the capital input types which may be employed. Manifestly, this tests credulity. Yet there is an additional problem of which account must be taken. As system (3-2) is written, there is no allowance for technical interaction among production subfunctions. The central idea here is that '. . . in fact, a large proportion of capital goods . . . perform interdependent functions' (Gort and Boddy, 1965, p. 395). *Inter alia*, 'technical interaction' contemplates the idea that '. . . there are strong logical and empirical grounds for believing direct technical linkages exist among the units forming a production complex' (Furubotn, 1970, p. 22). Indeed, the 'production complex' may contemplate a multi-plant firm where, for example, '. . . certain types of inputs can be attached to the complex as a whole rather than to any individual plant' (Furubotn, 1970, p. 23). It should be clear, therefore, that technical interaction contemplates a vast array of extant and potential interrelationships among capital stocks employed on a given 'plant floor', and among a single firm's multi-plant production facilities.

It is possible, in principle, to represent the technical interaction phenom-enon.[7] The effect is, of course, to expand further the array of production subfunctions available at a cross-section of time.

Manifestly, explicit recognition both of the (generally large) number of capital input types employed, and of the phenomenon of technical interaction forces attention upon an elementary fact: System (3-2), while heuristic, does not exhaustively represent the array of technical options available at a cross-section of time. Indeed, serious questions emerge as to whether the extent of the array--let alone the technical characteristics of each of the options--may be knowable (Roth, 1977).

The irremediable fact is that decision makers are boundedly, rather than classically rational. As has been emphasized, the technical constraints on choice include the properties of human beings as processors of information and as problem solvers (Simon, 1955, 1978).[8] As the discussion in Chapter 2 suggests, whereas classical rationality has, for decades, dominated economic modelling, 'the dominance is relaxing' (Conlisk, 1996, p. 669). There is, in fact, growing recognition that explicit account must be taken of decision maker's cognitive limitations, of the intervention in decision processes of short- and long-term memories, and of the propensity in the face of complexity to 'systematically restrict the use and acquisition of information compared to that potentially available' (Heiner, 1983, p. 564).[9]

The point at issue is not that it is impossible independently to secure evidence that decision makers are classically rational. Nor is it the point that there is a growing body of evidence in the experimental economics literature of 'anomalous behavior'; of behavior which is inconsistent with the classical rationality postulate. Rather, the point is that cognitive limitations both militate against optimizing solutions and account for a lack of correspondence between decision maker's objective and subjective decision environments. This phenomenon--characterized in Chapter 2 as the competence-difficulty or C-D gap--has as one of its corollaries uncertainty about how to use information in selecting potential actions. The structure of the uncertainty is, in turn, determined by 'environmental' and 'perceptual' variables (Heiner, 1983, pp. 564-565). Broadly speaking, the environmental variables determine the complexity of the decision problem, while the perceptual variables characterize the decision maker's 'competence in deciphering relationships between [his] behavior and the environment' (Heiner, 1983, p. 564).[10]

Bounded rationality in the sense of limited information processing ability may usefully be characterized as a defining characteristic of *homo sapiens* (as opposed to *homo economicus)*. Yet it is also true that the growth of knowledge is itself a source of a growing C-D gap

> . . . the generation of knowledge is also the generation of ignorance. The capacity of our brains to process the information available to them is challenged by the very productivity of the brain itself. . . .

> The difficulty of making intelligent decisions, whether personally or in an organization, has changed from ability to get information to one of processing a superabundance (Wilde, LeBaron and Israelsen, 1985, p. 407).

All of this has basic relevance to the 'choice of technique' problem. On the one hand, the number of available technical options, n, will, in many cases of practical importance, be unknowable. On the other hand, even if 'n' were known, it is unlikely that the firm will, at a cross-section of time, 'know' the engineering and other characteristics of each of the definable technical options.[11]   Indeed, there will be a divergence between the objective--but unknowable--decision environment, and its subjectively perceived counterpart. Whether, in addressing the C-D gap problem which inheres in the choice of technique problem the firm resorts to 'behavioral rules'--such as imitation, habit, or obeying an authority[12]-- is not the threshold issue. The essential point is that the juxtaposition of bounded rationality and the complexity of the choice of technique problem results, *pari passu*, in the absorption of decision costs. Understood to be a category of transaction costs (Furubotn and Richter, 1997, p. 31), decision costs arise when 'individuals incur costs in discovering options and choosing among them' (Furubotn and Richter, 1997, p. 452).

It is clear that the 'choice of technique' problem involves the absorption of decision costs. Yet, when decision makers are boundedly rational and decision costs are positive, a circularity problem arises

> This difficulty with strict optimization theory has become known as the 'circularity problem'--there does not exist an optimization problem which can be solved that fully incorporates the cost of decision making (Pingle, 1992, p. 10).

A corollary of this is an infinite regress problem

> There must come a point where the 'rational thing to do is to be irrational' and simply choose a choice method without reason. Otherwise, all resources would be used in decision-making (Pingle, 1992, p. 11).

The logic of the infinite regress problem does not simply call into question the constrained optimization paradigm. At a more fundamental level, it suggests that, in the face of complexity, decision makers may, indeed, resort to decision-cost minimizing choice methods. This has immediate relevance because the complexity of the choice of technique problem suggests that a producer is not likely to possess exhaustive knowledge of the available technical options and that, *pari passu*, only a subset of the available technical options will be considered. Granting this, 'the' production function may usefully be characterized as a subjectively determined technical array.[13] This is true from the perspective of one producer and, *pari passu*, from the perspective of all--boundedly rational--producers. Indeed, within an industry there can be no presumption that there will be a one-to-one correspondence among incumbent firms' (and prospective industry entrants') subjectively-determined technical arrays. This is a logical corollary of information asymmetry--another characteristic of observable reality. Finally, the methods of choosing among the subjectively perceived technical arrays may, themselves, be subjectively determined. *Inter alia*, each producer must decide whether: (1) To choose among the subset of technical options about which something is known--the *a priori* technical array--or (2) To choose among an expanded technical array; an array which includes technical options about which information has been acquired.[14]   The solution to these (and related) decision problems will be conditioned, in part, by intrinsically subjective prior stocks of knowledge, by decision makers' potentially disparate desiderata, and by the decision methods chosen by each producer.

While more can be said about this, the implication is clear: Even within an industry, there is no *a priori* reason to suppose that all producers will choose the same technical option. *Inter alia*, there can be no presumption that incumbent firms--or industry entrants--will employ the same differentiates of the capital input types typically employed within an industry. Granting this, there can be no presumption that the service flows employed across firms in the same industry will be technologically homogenous. Yet, if this is true within industries, it must, *mutatis mutandis*, be true across industries.

While the issue will be more fully explored in Chapter 4, the question at issue is, What are the implications for SWT? The central point is that the production-theoretic foundations of SWT contemplate the employment of production functions of the form specified by equation (3-1). Significantly, the inputs employed by all firms--within each, and across all industries--are technologically homogenous. Stated differently, whether the model contemplates two or m inputs, each firm is presumed to employ the same service flows. On this logic, the model suggests that a contract curve may be defined in input space. The contract curve is then employed to generate its output space analogue, the PPF. Finally, appeal to comparative static analysis results in the emergence of the Efficiency or Welfare Frontier.

The essential difficulty is that, once explicit account is taken of bounded rationality, of the growth of knowledge, and of positive decision costs, there can be no presumption that all firms will employ the same production function --let alone the same service flows. Once this has been said, it is clear that the space in which the contract curve might be defined is indeterminate. Stated differently, the logic of the firm-subjective production function militates against the specification of the contract curve defined in input space. It follows, *pari passu*, that the PPF cannot be defined. Insofar as the existence of the PPF is a *sine qua non* for the derivation of the Efficiency Frontier, the theoretical foundations of SWT are called into question. *Inter alia*, the logic of first-best Paretian optima--and therefore of competitive equilibria--is undermined. This, in turn, calls into question the efficacy of appeal to the efficiency standard.

The problem here is not equivalent to the nirvana fallacy. The fallacy obtains when the Efficiency Frontier is held up as a benchmark without taking account of one or more real and unavoidable constraints (Furubotn, 1994). The essential point here is that the firm-subjective nature of the production function militates against the specification of the benchmark Efficiency Frontier. It follows that the only evaluative standard to which SWT gives rise--the efficiency standard--is called into question.

Notes

1   See also Stigler, 1987, pp. 136-138; Roth, 1974.
2   At issue are the implications of individual generative assumptions, rather than the implications--designed or otherwise--of the model.
3   For more on this, see Roth, 1973; Roth, 1974.
4   Interestingly, the neoclassical long-run expansion path [LREP] is intended to represent the 'long-run' decision environment; a situation in which capital stocks and, *pari passu*, the production function change. Yet, as movement along the LREP proceeds, the production function does *not* change.
5   See also Furubotn, 1965, pp. 295-296.
6   For more on the stock-flow production function, see Roth, 1979.
7   See Furubotn, 1970, pp. 22-28; Roth, 1972, p. 251.
8   See, especially, Simon, 1966, pp. 19-20.
9   Professor Conlisk proffers four reasons for incorporating bounded rationality in economic models (1996, p. 669). For more on bounded rationality, see Roth, 1998.
10   See also Miller, 1983, p. 45.
11   The intertemporal problem is manifestly more difficult. Allowance must be made, not only for endogenously generated technological change, but for asymmetric information diffusion and other path-dependencies.
12   See Heiner, 1983, pp. 585-586; Pingle, 1992, p. 8.
13   See Furubotn, 1970; Roth, 1972.
14   For an approach to this problem, see Roth, 1977.

4 The Implications for the Efficiency Frontier

4.1 The Theoretical Foundations of the Frontier

As has been suggested, 'high-brow economics'--the body of social welfare (and social choice) theory--takes as its point of departure 'everyone pursuing their self-interest, given tastes and technology' (Klamer, 1989, p. 147). Chapters 2 and 3 have codified in somewhat more detail the essential features of the decision environment contemplated by the underlying, neoclassical theory. Emphasis has been placed on the empirical, logical and other difficulties which attend the 'frictionless' decision environment envisioned by the standard theory. The imprimatur of instrumentalist methodology notwithstanding, the systematic employment of unrealistic generative assumptions both denies the relevance of fundamental features of observable reality and results in the emergence of logical conundra. *Inter alia*, the inability to test for stability of preferences independent of the classical rationality postulate means that the neoclassical theory of choice can neither be confirmed nor disconfirmed. For its part, the key auxiliary assumption embedded in neoclassical production theory, fixed technology, is irreconcilable with a generative assumption, perfect adaptability.

The essential point is that the comparative simplicity and elegance of intendedly value-free and frictionless neoclassical theory is achieved at considerable cost. At the most rudimentary level, neoclassical theory's claim to be a part of the corpus of empirical science is undermined by the non-testability of one of its components, and by the logical inconsistencies inherent in another. If nothing else were said, the case for fundamental revision of the received theory's key behavioral and technological postulates will have been made. Yet more can, and must, be said. The core idea is that

All economic phenomena must be understood to be embedded in an environment in which costly transactions, incomplete information, and bounded rationality rule everywhere (Furubotn, 1994, p. 13).

This idea is a recurring theme of Chapters 2 and 3. It remains now to adduce the implications of an explicit accounting of these phenomena for SWT; in particular, for the Efficiency Frontier.

4.2 The Assumption Set Revised: The Consumer

As was suggested in Chapter 2, the individual's preference structure cannot adequately be represented by an intertemporally stable, single-equation utility function. *Inter alia*, path-dependencies are a palpable reality. Their existence rules out the analytically convenient assumptions that preference--and value-- structures are both constant and exogenously determined. While more will be said about this in Chapter 6, immediate interest centers on the emerging litera- ture on preference domains. As was emphasized in Chapter 2, the literature suggests that internal conflict is a defining characteristic of cognitive processes. In effect, individual preference systems involve a number of preference domains, each of which is representable by a utility subfunction. Characteristically, the arguments of a number of these subfunctions will include goods and services. But the presumption must be that one or more of the subfunctions contemplate arguments which are broadly reflective of society's view of acceptable behavior; of how the individual 'ought' to behave. In effect, the individual's utility domains incorporate both tastes and values (or moral tastes). As Professor Buchanan has observed

> . . . the attempted separation between economics and morals was, at best, an illusion that simply cannot be sustained. Economics models persons as maximizers of utility, but arguments in utility functions include rules that restrict the range of choices that are made (Buchanan, 1994a, p. 128).

The notion that ethical norms 'restrict the range of choices that are made' is both self-evident and important. It is important, *inter alia*, because a world characterized by bounded rationality and information asymmetries is con- ducive to opportunistic behavior. The resultant, positive transaction costs can be mitigated by the intervention of ethical constraints on behavior.

Resistance to an explicit accounting of such interrelationships is, of course, animated by the notion that neoclassical and, *pari passu*, SWT are positivist in orientation and in execution. Yet, as was suggested in Chapter 1, SWT is a hybrid moral theory. On the one hand

> . . . the standard definition of a social optimum compares social alternatives exclusively in terms of the goodness of outcomes (rather than the rightness of their procedures) and identifies the goodness of outcomes with satisfaction of individual preferences. These commitments to value only outcomes and to measure outcomes only in terms of individual utilities are neither neutral nor uncontroversial. . . . (Hausman and McPherson, 1993, p. 675).

On the other hand, unattenuated exchange and property rights are instrumentally important to the achievement of first-best Paretian optima (Chapters 1 and 5).[1] It follows that SWT embodies elements of goal- and rights-based moral theories.

Given that SWT is a hybrid moral theory, the failure to take explicit account of the role and importance of ethical norms is, at best, logically inconsistent. Yet an explicit accounting of ethical norms implicates the notion of utility domains and, *mutatis mutandis*, abandonment of the single-equation conception of the utility function. While appeal to a multi-equation utility construct facilitates the modelling of internal conflict, and of utility domains generally, the analytical price is high: *Inter alia*, the familiar logic of contract curve derivation is compromised. Even if it were assumed that each individual's preference and value structure is defined over the same utility domains, the space in which contract curves (hyperplanes) might be derived is indeterminate. Yet the interaction of bounded rationality, information asymmetries and path-dependencies would seem to ensure that individuals will be characterized by disparate preference and value domains.[2] Once this has been said, the arguments of utility subfunctions will differ across individuals. It follows that the contract curves which are a *sine qua non* for the derivation of the Efficiency Frontier are indeterminate.

This conclusion is reinforced once account is taken of the complex nature of individuals' desiderata. The problem is not simply that individuals' preference and value domains are heterogeneous. Indeed, the problem would persist even if it were assumed that preference and value domains were homogeneous across individuals. This, in turn, is a corollary of another fundamental feature of observable reality: Each product type, X_i, i = 1, 2, . . ., n typically appears in differentiated forms. Product type X_1, for example, may appear in s differentiated forms. Granting this, individuals have choice among the various differentiates, X_{1j}, j = 1, 2, . . . , s, of product type one. The same is true, *mutatis mutandis*, of the differentiates of the n-1 other product types.

The essential idea is that the array of goods extant at a cross section of time may be distinguished by their technical characteristics, by their associated property rights bundles, and by their ethical attributes (both in use and in acquisition).[3] In effect, each differentiate of each product type is possessed of a vector of characteristics, some of which are subjectively perceived. In such a world there can be no presumption that, for any two individuals, the 'goods' appearing as arguments in their respective utility subfunctions will be the same. Indeed, in a world characterized by an array of objectively and subjectively distinguishable differentiates of an indefinitely large number of product types there can be no presumption that a boundedly rational individual knows the number, let alone the objectively determinable characteristics, of the goods and services which confront him. In effect, the goods which appear as arguments of an individual's utility subfunctions must be understood to consist in a subjectively perceived subset of the goods and services actually available.[4] Add to this the empirical reality of the emergence of new product types, and of new differentiates of extant product types, and the presumption must be that, for any individual, there can be no one-to-one correspondence between his objectively defined and subjectively perceived decision environments. Moreover, given that boundedly rational individuals are characterized both by differing stocks of knowledge and by differing abilities to process extant and new information, it follows that subjectively perceived decision environments will differ across individuals. A corollary of this is that boundedly rational individuals will, at a cross section of time, be possessed of heterogenous multi-equation utility functions. Each multi-equation system will, in turn, be defined on disparate preference and value domains, and on differing, subjectively determined subsets of the available goods and services.

Whatever else is said, it is clear that these considerations militate against the derivation of contract curves in 'goods' space. Given that the space in which the requisite contract curves might be derived is indeterminate, it follows, *pari passu*, that the Efficiency Frontier cannot be derived. As has been suggested, the problem here goes beyond the oft-cited nirvana fallacy. The fallacy obtains when the Efficiency Frontier is held up as a benchmark without taking explicit account of one or more real and unavoidable constraints (Furubotn, 1994). The complexities outlined here suggest that the Efficiency Frontier cannot meaningfully be defined.[5]

While a fuller discussion is deferred to Chapter 6, the complex decision environment envisioned here has implications for the Social Welfare Function. In particular, once allowance is made for preference endogeneity, for path dependencies, and for meddlesome or nosy preferences, an intertemporal inter-personal utility comparison (IUC) problem emerges for the same individual.[6] Manifestly, this complicates the basic IUC problem; namely, 'the heterogeneity of men, the variance of their preferences and capacities for satisfaction'

(Rothschild, 1993, p. 89). While it is possible to conceive of strategies which will allow for some generalizations regarding IUCs, each is subject to daunting technical problems.[7] Unless these problems can be resolved--something which appears to be unlikely--Arrow's impossibility result will retain its basic relevance (Arrow, 1951, p. 59). This line of argument suggests that the complexities which call into question the existence of the Efficiency Frontier also militate against the construction of a meaningful Social Welfare Function. Finally, as will be emphasized in Chapter 6, the juxtaposition of meddlesome or nosy preferences and respect for individual liberty may rule out the possibility of any social choice.[8]

Granting the logic of what has been said, an explicit accounting of observable features of reality undermines the utility-theoretic foundations of both the Efficiency Frontier and the Social Welfare Function. While discussion of the latter is deferred to Chapter 6, the issue of immediate interest is, Does an explicit accounting of observable features of reality compromise the production-theoretic foundation of SWT?

4.3 The Assumption Set Revised: The Producer

The point of departure of Chapter 3 is that the single-equation neoclassical production function provides the technological foundation of SWT. Reduced to its essentials, the derivation of the orthodox production possibility frontier (PPF) depends upon a particular understanding of the producer's decision environment. *Inter alia*, 'the' production function is assumed to be 'output maximizing' or 'efficient'. This assumption, in turn, requires that, in the short run, the capital stock which generates the fixed service flow, x_2^0, be 'perfectly adaptable'; that it adapt itself instantaneously and costlessly to changing rates of use of the variable service flow, x_1.

Emphasis was placed in Chapter 2 on the notion that, while positive or instrumentalist methodology endorses the employment of unrealistic generative assumptions, logical inconsistences are (or should be) inadmissible. Difficulties arise precisely because the perfect adaptability assumption implies that, as movement along the short-run expansion path (SREP) proceeds, the capital stock which generates the fixed service flow 'has unique and optimal physical form in each combination' (Furubotn, 1964, p. 22). Yet the instantaneous and costless 'metamorphosis' of the capital stock implies that the technical properties of the 'fixed' service flow must change. It follows, *pari passu*, that as adaptation proceeds, the production function changes, and movement along the SREP is a technological impossibility. This logical conundrum has implications for SWT.

The essential point is that the implicit assumption that the production function is invariant with respect to changes in the physical and therefore technical properties of capital stocks denies a fundamental feature of observable reality: The technological link between outputs and inputs is, by definition, an engineering phenomenon. Yet it is well known that choice among differentiated forms of capital input types implies a choice among alternative production functions. Given this understanding, 'the' production function is, in fact, a multi-equation construct, with each production subfunction capable of producing the desired output flow. A corollary of this is that the producer confronts a 'choice of technique' problem; a problem which is complicated by the fact that, in virtually all cases of practical importance, the array of competing production subfunctions is large. Indeed, from the perspective of the boundedly rational producer, the array may be indefinitely large. Moreover, knowledge of the technical properties of each--or even a subset--of the available subfunctions is constrained by the intervention of 'environmental' and 'perceptual' variables; by the complexity of the decision problem itself, and by the competence of the decision maker (Heiner, 1983, pp. 564-565).

In the face of these complexities, the choice of technique problem involves the absorption of decision costs; costs which, *inter alia*, give rise to an infinite regress problem, the resolution of which involves choosing a choice method without reason (Pingle, 1992, pp. 10-11). A corollary of this is that, in contrast to the neoclassical paradigm, there can be no presumption that producers in the same industry--let alone all industries--will employ the same productive service flows. In effect, the essential heterogeneity of boundedly rational decision makers ensures the heterogeneity of their subjectively-determined production functions. The intervention of differing prior stocks of knowledge, of path-dependencies (including learning, experience, habits, and the application of rules-of-thumb), and of differing abilities to process extant and new information is an irremediable fact; a fact which militates against the simultaneous employment, at a cross-section of time, of the same production function by all producers. Add to this the intertemporal phenomenon of technological change and the asymmetric diffusion of new technical knowledge and it is clear that the rarefied decision environment contemplated by neoclassical production theory has no operational counterpart. Whereas the frictionless neoclassical world envisions the employment of technologically homogeneous service flows within and across industries, the explicit introduction of 'frictions' ensures technological heterogeneity across firms. In effect, the firm-subjective production function is a defining characteristic of a world characterized by bounded rationality and positive transaction costs.

The logic of the firm-subjective production function has basic relevance to the body of received SWT. As is well known, generation of the Efficiency Frontier is predicated, in part, on the existence of the production possibility frontier (PPF). Yet the logic of the PPF requires, *inter alia*, that all producers --both within and across industries--employ the same inputs. This, as we have seen, is irreconcilable with a technical environment characterized by cognitive limits, information asymmetries and positive transaction (decision) costs. Reduced to its essentials, the employment of subjectively-determined production functions--and, *pari passu*, of technologically heterogenous service flows--militates against the derivation of the PPF. This, in turn, means that it is not possible to effect a mapping of utility possibility frontiers and, *pari passu*, the Grand Utility Possibility or Efficiency Frontier. In effect, the intrinsic firm-subjectivity of the underlying production functions renders the Efficiency Frontier indeterminate.[9]

4.4 The Indeterminacy of the Efficiency Frontier

The argument developed to this point reduces to this: The conceptual under-pinnings of the new SWT contemplate a rarefied, 'frictionless' decision environment for which no empirical counterpart exists. Yet, once account is taken of some fundamental features of observable reality, the logic of the Efficiency Frontier is called into question. The irremediable fact is that the complexity of the resultant decision environment militates against the theo-retical derivation of the Frontier. Stated differently, once allowance is made for bounded rationality and positive transaction costs, the Efficiency Frontier is indeterminate. This, in turn, has implications for the efficiency standard and, *pari passu*, for the conduct of public policy.

4.5 The Implications for Public Policy

As is well known, points on the Efficiency Frontier constitute first-best Pareto optimal or 'efficient' configurations. The logic of the efficiency standard is captured by the first and second fundamental welfare theorems. The first theorem asserts that, under certain simplifying assumptions, a competitive capitalist system will automatically move to a first-best, Pareto-optimal equilibrium (Novshek and Sonnenschein, 1987; Duffie and Sonnenschein, 1989). Characteristically, the 'simplifying assumptions' contemplate, *inter alia*, classical rationality, zero transaction costs, 'pure-rental type' firms, and an institutionless decision environment (Furubotn and Richter, 1991, pp. 11-12). For its part, the second welfare theorem indicates that, no matter to which point on the Efficiency Frontier a perfectly competitive economy is (automatically) impelled, a different, 'socially desired', Pareto-efficient allocation can be realized through the use of lump-sum taxes and bounties (Graaff, 1967, pp. 75-83). On this logic, the efficacy of the (perfectly competitive) market mechanism is preserved

> The [second welfare] theorem is widely interpreted as meaning that we can divorce the issue of efficiency from distribution. It is not an argument against markets that the resulting distribution of income is undesirable. If society does not like the distribution of income, the government's distribution branch . . . just alters the initial endowment of resources, through lump-sum redistributions (Stiglitz, 1994, p. 45).

While much can be said about this, three points merit particular emphasis: (1) Even if the logic of the underlying theory were granted, lump-sum measures are 'extraordinarily hard to devise' (Graaff, 1967, p. 78). (2) It is significant--and, it might be argued, anomalous--that an intendedly value-free and institutionless theory is employed to rationalize a governmental 'distribution branch'. I shall return to this issue in Chapter 8. (3) Once allowance is made for bounded rationality, for positive transaction costs and for other fundamental features of observable reality, the Efficiency Frontier is indeterminate. It follows, *pari passu*, that the first and second welfare theorems no longer have basic relevance, and appeal to the classic marginal equivalences needed for Pareto optimality is unavailing. The unavoidable conclusion is that the efficiency standard cannot serve as a useful guide for public policy formulation.[10]

Insofar as it is the only evaluative standard to which the theory gives rise, the indeterminancy of the efficiency standard raises fundamental questions about the usefulness of SWT. These questions are further animated when attention focuses on the irreconcilability of the consequentialist or goal-based efficiency standard with respect for the rights which social welfare theorists regard as instrumentally important to the achievement of first-best Paretian optima.

Perhaps because of their propensity to engage in intendedly value-free analysis, economists have paid relatively little attention to alternative rights construals, to their associated, correlative duties, and to the implications for SWT. This is true, even among economists who regard 'freedom' as morally exigent. This is the subject matter of Chapter 5.

Notes

1   The path to first-best Paretian optima under a competitive system is also commonly understood to be facilitated by the zero transaction cost assumption. However, contrary to the conventional wisdom, the assumption leads to a logical conundrum. Reduced to its essentials, a decision environment characterized by zero transaction costs is congenial to the formation of coalitions which, effectively, rule out the satisfaction of the conditions for a Pareto optimum. See Furubotn, 1991.
2   This conclusion is reinforced when account is taken of the disparate effects on preference and value structures of heterogeneous cultures.
3   See Buchanan, 1994a, p. 134; Furubotn and Pejovich, 1974; Roth, 1975.
4   See Furubotn, 1994; Roth, 1975.
5   Robert Frank has observed that it is not clear '. . . how even to *define* an efficiency standard when individual preferences are highly malleable' (1996, p. 119; emphasis in original). See also Furubotn, 1994.
6   The phenomena of learning and asymmetric information diffusion have basic relevance here. For a discussion of the process of information diffusion, see Furubotn, 1994.
7   See Rothschild, 1993.
8   See Sen, 1995; Hausman and McPherson, 1993, p. 716.
9   Professor Furubotn has shown that, 'even when taken on its own narrow terms, the standard [neoclassical flow-flow production function] gives a misleading view of valid production possibilities'. *Inter alia*, the failure to take explicit account of the relationships among the *intensity* of input usage, input prices and productivity results in an inappropriate delimitation of the firm's technical options. Once account is taken of these interrelationships, and given that the firm's desideratum is profit maximization, 'unvarying output maximization cannot be an enterprise policy' (1997, p. 4). Moreover, 'the failure to establish a more comprehensive representation of the technical options means . . . that [the firm] will not achieve a Pareto-optimal factor allocation'. A corollary of this is that 'the use of the neoclassical production function is, in general, inconsistent with the possibility of an economy reaching an ideal competitive equilibrium' (1997, p.5).
10 See, for example, Furubotn and Richter, 1991, p. 12; Frank, 1996, p. 119.

5 Efficiency and Rights

5.1 Introduction

At the risk of some redundancy, it is important to emphasize that logical positivism is the methodological position of choice among neoclassical economists. It follows, *pari passu*, that neoclassical theory and its derivative, SWT, are institutionless and intendedly value-free.[1] We have seen, however, that SWT is not value-free. Indeed, SWT is, demonstrably, an example of a consequentialist moral theory. The essential point is that 'social optima' contemplate social alternatives defined in terms of the goodness of outcomes, rather than in terms of the rightness of procedures. Moreover, the goodness of outcomes is identified with the satisfaction of individual preferences. While the desiderata upon which preferences are based are, in principle, unspecified, the essence of first-best Paretian optima is that no one can be made 'better off' without someone else being made 'worse off'. It is in this sense that SWT is a part of the corpus of consequentialist moral theory.

While it is apparent that many economists have failed to recognize--or chosen to ignore--the ethical content of SWT, my interest in this chapter centers on a related problem. Perhaps because it is intendedly value-free, the proponents of SWT have generally failed explicitly to deal either with the normative content or the implications of their commitment to 'freedom'

> It is ironic that welfare economics focuses almost exclusively on the Pareto efficiency concepts. For economists typically value freedom; and much of the traditional case for capitalism was not so much in terms of its capacity to 'deliver the goods' as in terms of the protection that the separation of economic and political power offers to individual liberty. . . . (Hausman and McPherson, 1993, p. 693).[2]

Characteristically, social welfare theorists, like most economists, regard 'freedom' as intrinsically valuable; as morally exigent in itself. Moreover, social welfare theorists assign (unattenuated) exchange and property rights an instrumental role in the achievement of first-best Paretian optima. That said, social welfare theory's proponents have generally failed to recognize that the

35

sanctioned rights to which they assign an instrumental role cannot, in the context of consequentialist SWT, have moral force. As we shall see, the problem is that the rights which are regarded as instrumentally important and, therefore, as legally justified, need not, in consequentialist theory, be respected.

The failure to recognize--or, perhaps, to acknowledge--the fundamental irreconcilability of consequentialist theory and the moral force of rights has profound implications for SWT. The difficulty is that, even if one grants its existence, the path to the Efficiency Frontier is not assured. Simply stated, the duties which are correlative to the implicitly sanctioned rights--the obligation not to violate others' exchange and property rights--may, in consequentialist times, be overcome by purely utilitarian considerations. In the face of this conundrum, a fundamental question arises: Is the only evaluative standard to which SWT gives rise, efficiency, a suitable guide to public policy formulation? For reasons discussed below, and in earlier chapters, I argue that it is not.

5.2 The Treatment of Rights

Amartya Sen has observed that '. . . Pareto efficiency . . . takes no direct note of anything other than utilities (such as rights or freedom) beyond their indirect role in generating utilities' (1995, p. 3). While this may be ascribed to a methodological commitment to 'scientific' or value-free welfare economics, the disinclination to assign rights lexical priority[3] may also reflect the fact that '. . . [rights] appear to be unacceptable to utilitarians since they impede the unfettered pursuit of the social good' (Almond, 1993, p. 266). In any case, while rights and liberties play no direct role in the evaluation of states-of-affairs, they do assume an implicit, instrumental role in SWT. As we have seen, unfettered exchange and property rights are a *sine qua non* for the achievement of first-best Paretian optima. Beyond this, social welfare theorists' commitment to the primacy of autonomous, atomistic and narrowly self-interested decision-making has meant that

> Rights have been seen as a basis of protection not for all human interests but for those specifically related to choice, self-determination, agency and independence. On this view, the duties correlative to rights are mainly negative in character: They are duties to refrain from obstructing action or interfering with choice; rather than duties to provide assistance. This understanding is related . . . to principles of laissez-faire and minimalist theories of the state (Waldron, 1995, p. 11).

On this account, rights are instrumentally important both because of their role in the achievement of efficient or Pareto-optimal outcomes,[4] and because laissez-faire and minimalist government are consonant with 'choice, self-determination, agency and independence'.[5]

5.3　Rights, Duties and Utilitarian Social Welfare Theory

'Rights', no matter how construed, are associated with correlative duties.[6] At issue, at least for present purposes, is whether a right carries with it the moral obligation to respect it. With this as the point of departure, it must be understood that there are three ways in which the 'special force of rights' may be understood

(1)　a right is nothing but a particularly important interest. While it is assigned a greater weight than ordinary interests it can, in principle, be outweighed;

(2)　the interests protected by rights may be given what John Rawls has called lexical priority over other interests.[7] Such interests are to be protected (and promoted) to the greatest extent possible before other interests are taken into consideration. *Inter alia*, this makes rights absolute against considerations of 'mere utility';

(3)　rights are not construed as lexically weighted interests. Rather, they serve as the basis of 'strict constraining requirements on action' (Waldron, 1995, p. 15).[8]

It is apparent that the understanding of the 'special force of rights' which has basic relevance to utilitarian SWT is the first:

The violation or fulfillment of basic liberties or rights tends to be ignored in traditional utilitarian welfare economics not just because of its consequentialist focus, but particularly because of its 'welfarism', whereby consequent states of affairs are judged exclusively by the utilities generated in the respective states (Sen, 1995, p. 13).

This formulation is important, both for what it tells us about the 'lack of force' of rights in SWT, and for its emphasis on the utilitarian nature of the theory.

Broadly speaking, SWT is accommodative of two forms of utilitarianism.[9] The first, 'preference' utilitarianism, contemplates preference satisfaction. For preference utilitarians and, it would seem, for most social welfare theorists, there is no presumption that individuals should have particular preferences. Rather, preference utilitarianism asserts that 'It is good--good for them--to have their preferences satisfied, whatever their preferences may be' (Goodin, 1993, p. 243). In contrast, 'welfare' utilitarians 'would suppress short-sighted preference satisfaction in favor of protecting people's long-term welfare interests' (Goodin, 1993, p. 244).[10] From the perspective of SWT, the essential point is, however, that 'Utilitarianism of whatever stripe is, first and foremost, a standard for judging public action. . . .' (Goodin, 1993, p. 245). And, from the perspective of public policy, '. . . . the right action is that which maximizes utility (however construed) summed impersonally across all those affected by that action' (Goodin, 1993, p. 245). It follows, *pari passu*, that for traditional utilitarian welfare economics

> . . . only consequences for individual well-being matter, with other items such as rights or virtues viewed strictly as means to promoting welfare (Hausman and McPherson, 1993, p. 704).

This understanding of the 'special force of rights' contrasts sharply with the libertarian view. From the libertarian perspective, rights are not merely lexically weighted interests. Rather, rights--which determine the distribution of freedom--serve as 'strict constraining requirements on action'. Since, for libertarians, 'the point of rights . . . is to secure liberty . . . considerations of welfare never justify interferences with individual liberty' (Hausman and McPherson, 1993, p. 704).[11]

While this view of rights as absolute side constraints on action[12] appears clearly to be irreconcilable with utilitarian SWT, some have suggested that SWT may be reconcilable with a view of rights as intrinsically valuable. Amartya Sen has argued, for example, that "The need to guarantee some 'minimal liberties' on a priority basis can be incorporated in social choice formulations" (1995, p. 13). The idea is to embed rights protections--or rights violations or losses of liberty--in 'states of affairs' or consequences.

As it happens, this approach cannot capture the view of rights as morally exigent in themselves

> This approach seems to capture only part of the value of rights-protection. For, in a situation in which committing one . . . wrong, such as torturing a child, will

prevent others from perpetrating two equally serious wrongs, this approach would mandate carrying out the torture. But many would say that such actions are wrong, regardless of the consequences. . . . The consequentialist view does not capture the sense that the moral imperative on me is that I should not torture the child (Hausman and McPherson, 1993, pp. 695-696).

It is clear then, then, that consequentialist SWT is incompatible with the view that rights are intrinsically valuable; that they are morally exigent in themselves. Given that intrinsically valuable rights cannot be accommodated, it follows that the correlative duty not to violate such rights cannot be accommodated. The essential difficulty is that, 'Like rights, obligations have a normative life of their own, with implications that are neither reducible to, nor traceable by, direct considerations of utility' (Lyons, 1982, p. 133).[13] Moreover, this objection applies with equal force to rule-utilitarianism. Whether in preference or welfare form, rule-utilitarianism

. . . limits the application of the standard of utility to rules or social institutions and requires compliance with rules that are certified as having the requisite utilitarian justification (Lyons, 1982, p. 128).

Insofar as the rules or social institutions requiring compliance contemplate duties to respect intrinsically valuable rights, it would appear that rule-utilitarianism can accommodate the moral force of rights. There is, however, a logical problem: If a utilitarian believes that certain rules are justified on utilitarian grounds, he does not contradict himself 'by supposing that direct utilitarian arguments for deviating from the rules may be entertained' (Lyons, 1982, p. 129). It follows, *pari passu*, that the rule-utilitarian '. . . cannot regard the morally defensible rights under utilitarian institutions as having moral force' (Lyons, 1982, p. 129).[14]

Granting the logic of what has been said, it is clear that utilitarian SWT is irreconcilable with the moral force of rights and their correlative duties. Manifestly, this means that respect for the exchange and property rights which are instrumental to the achievement of efficient or Pareto optimal outcomes is not assured. It follows that, even if the logical, empirical and other difficulties outlined in earlier chapters were overcome, a competitive system would not necessarily be impelled to a point on its Efficiency Frontier. That this is so follows from the fact that instrumentally important rights and correlative duties might not be respected. Yet, paradoxically, a similar problem emerges when, under plausible conditions, minimal liberty *is* respected.

Consider a decision environment in which persons possess what Sen (1976) has characterized as 'meddlesome' or 'nosy' preferences. If, in the elementary two-person case, one person cares about the other's consumption pattern--a plausible state-of-affairs[15]--and personal liberty *is* respected, then

> . . . if one strengthens Sen's minimal liberty condition to permit two individuals to be decisive over all pairs of alternatives which differ with respect to purely personal matters, . . . certain combinations of preferences will rule out the possibility of any social choice. . . . (Hausman and McPherson, 1993, p. 716).

The problem here is not that rights might *not* be respected. The 'impossibility of the Paretian liberal' arises because rights might be respected.[16] Amartya Sen summarizes the situation this way

> The 'impossibility of the Paretian liberal' captures the conflict between (i) the special importance of a person's preferences over his own personal sphere, and (ii) the general importance of people's preferences over any choice regardless of field (1995, p. 13).

It is clear that the inability to attain 'efficient' solutions is attributable here to a particular understanding of the special force of rights. Here, rights are construed as a side constraint on social choice. While Nozick (1974) and other libertarians have argued that, while rights are, properly, to be given priority, Sen's paradox arises because of a misconstrual of rights. The argument reduces to the notion that, while having a 'privacy' right permits one to do as he pleases, it does not permit a person to be decisive over social choices.[17] Others have argued that rights might be modelled as 'game forms', rather than as side constraints on action or social choice (Gibbard, 1974). The idea here is that individuals could, in principle, enter into trades or contracts which would facilitate the attainment of Pareto optimal outcomes.

There are, however, at least two objections to the 'game form solution'. First, one might plausibly ask how such contracting could be reconciled with the 'frictionless' decision environment contemplated by SWT. Presumptively, such contracting would contemplate positive transaction costs. In effect, the parties would absorb *ex ante* and *ex post* monitoring costs.[18] Second, Basu (1984) and Riley (1989) have shown that, where rights and efficiency or Pareto optimality conflict, the outcomes which respect rights are not Nash equilibria.[19] Such solutions are not Pareto optimal.[20]

The conclusion which emerges is that there appears to be no way to respect rights and, at the same time, to achieve efficient outcomes. As Sen has observed

> The 'ways out' that have been sought have varied between (i) weakening the priority of liberties (thereby qualifying the minimal liberty condition), (ii) constraining the field-independent force of preferences (thereby qualifying the Pareto principle), and (iii) restricting the domain of permissible individual preference profiles (Sen, 1995, p. 13).

While the first two 'ways out' plainly underscore the irreconcilability of respect for rights and Pareto optimality, the third effectively rules out a fundamental feature of observable reality. As Professor Buchanan has observed

> Each of us is concerned about the preferences, the utility functions, of others than ourselves. And to say this is not to say that each of us have 'meddlesome' preferences (Sen, 1976). . . . I cannot rationally remain indifferent to your preferences if your choices do, indeed, affect my economic well-being (1994b, p. 75).[21]

In sum, it appears that there is no 'way out'. The impossibility of the Paretian liberal 'persists under virtually every plausible concept of individual rights' (Gaertner, Pattanaik and Suzumura, 1992).

There is, finally, one residual issue. Some have argued that the libertarians' conception of the special force of rights is inappropriate. On this view, preference-independent, consequence-detached rights are inadmissible

> . . . in deciding on what rights to protect and codify, and in determining how the underlying purpose might be most effectively achieved, there is a need to look at the likely consequences of different game-form specifications, and to relate them to what people value and desire (Sen, 1995, p. 14).

Professor Sen's motivating example contemplates an externality: Smoking in a public place leads 'unwilling victims' to inhale others' smoke. The presumption is that, under these circumstances, a case could be made for modifying a game-form so that smoking is banned. In effect, the argument is that rights may be derived from consequences.

There are at least two problems with the suggested approach. First, Sen's motivating example assumes the right he argues might be derived from the consequence: '. . . --it is assumed--[the unwilling victims] have a right to avoid (inhaling others' smoke)' (Sen, 1995, p. 15). Second, the approach employs consequential analysis "(in an 'inverse form': from consequences to antecedents)" (Sen, 1995, p. 15). The fact that the antecedent which Sen wishes to derive is a right leads, however, to a logical conundrum: '. . . rights . . . have a normative life of their own, with implications that are neither reducible to, nor traceable by, direct considerations of utility' (Lyons, 1982, p. 133).[22] Simply stated, rights cannot be derived from consequences.

The conclusions which emerge from this analysis are, therefore, that:

(1) Utilitarian--and, therefore, consequentialist--SWT cannot regard the rights which are instrumentally important to the achievement of first-best Paretian optima as having moral force.

(2) Embedding morally exigent rights in consequences or states-of-affairs captures only a part of the value of rights-protection. Moreover, the correlative duty to not violate such rights cannot, in consequentialist terms, have moral force. Finally the 'impossibility of the Paretian liberal' militates against the accommodation of minimal 'privacy' rights.

(3) Consequentialist analysis cannot be employed in 'inverse form' to determine antecedent rights.

The corollary of these considerations is that

> Economists . . . are thus faced with a significant theoretical decision. Either they shall consider efficiency the sole fundamental basis for normative appraisal . . . or they must accept the idea that there are other values to be served beyond economic efficiency, in which case they must entertain the possibility of rights and obligations that are independent of social recognition and enforcement, rights and obligations that justified legal institutions ought to respect (Lyons, 1982, p. 128).

The issue here is not the existence of the Efficiency Frontier. As we saw in earlier chapters, the Frontier is, in fact, indeterminate. Nor is the issue the question of the idea of 'social preference'.[23] This question is deferred to Chapter 7. Rather, the issue is the irreconcilability of 'efficiency' and respect for instrumentally important and/or intrinsically valuable rights.

The root cause of the problem is the 'hybrid' nature of SWT. On the one hand, the theory is predicated on received, neoclassical theory. Emphasis is therefore placed on the primacy of unboundedly rational, atomistic, autonomous, and narrowly self-interested behavior. On the other hand, economic policy appraisals invoke a consequentialist evaluative standard--efficiency--which is predicated on a nonindividuated, collective goal, the constrained maximization of aggregative welfare. And, has been repeatedly emphasized, a *sine qua non* for the achievement of efficient outcomes is respect for instrumentally important exchange and property rights.

The essential point is that social welfare theorists implicitly assume that two distinct moral theories are reconcilable: (1) Given the implicit role of instrumentally important rights--and given the view of most economists that 'freedom' is morally exigent--SWT incorporates elements of rights-based moral theories. (2) Given that it is formulated in preference, welfare or in rule-utilitarian form, SWT is a consequentialist or goal-based moral theory.[24] The problem, as we have seen, is that rights- and goal-based moral theories are not reconcilable:

> . . . utilitarian arguments for institutional design (the arguments that utilitarians might use in favor of establishing or maintaining certain legal rights) do not logically or morally exclude direct utilitarian arguments concerning the exercise of, or interference with such rights. As a consequence, evaluation of conduct from a utilitarian standpoint is dominated by direct utilitarian arguments and therefore ignores the moral force of justified legal rights (Lyons, 1982, p. 113).[25]

What has been suggested reduces to this: Given its hybrid nature, SWT is internally inconsistent. In the face of this conundrum, social welfare theorists must either argue that the rights which they regard as instrumentally important are morally exigent in themselves (and reject the efficiency standard), or embrace the efficiency standard and deny the moral force of rights.[26] The latter approach is, of course, difficult to reconcile with most economists' predilection to value freedom and the rights which determine its distribution (Hayek, 1960; Friedman, 1962). Presumptively, for these economists, rights are morally exigent in themselves. Yet, even if this were not true, most economists would agree that 'A market economy is perhaps best viewed as a network of rights and obligations based on contracts and legal requirements' (Furubotn and Richter, 1997, p. 40).[27] In short, economists who regard rights as intrinsically valuable and/or as instrumentally important cannot, at the same time, embrace the efficiency standard.

Notes

1   The same might be said of some theoretical constructs in sociology, psychology and political science. See, for example, Miller, 1997; Lewin, 1996; Baron and Hannan, 1994.
2   See also Waldron, 1995, p. 11.
3   For a discussion of lexical ordering, see Rawls, 1971, pp. 42-43.
4   For a discussion of the nature and importance of property rights, see Furubotn and Pejovich, 1974, esp. p. 4. See also Furubotn and Pejovich, 1972.

5   See also Almond, 1993, p. 260; Hausman and McPherson, 1993, p. 695.

6   What has been styled the 'most celebrated taxonomy of rights' is found in Hohfeld, 1919.

7   Here, the interests protected by rights are given priority in serial or lexical order. Such an ordering 'requires us to satisfy the first principle in the ordering before we can move on to the second, . . . , and so on' (Rawls, 1971, pp. 42-43).

8   For a discussion of rights as 'trumps' see Dworkin, 1978, esp. pp. 82-90; Dworkin, 1995.

9   'Rule-utilitarianism' may take the form of preference or welfare utilitarianism. I shall have more to say about this below. For a discussion of Bentham's hedonic or psychological utilitarianism, see Dworkin, 1978, p. 233. This form of utilitarianism is only rarely invoked.

10   The notion of welfare interests is predicated on the idea that it is possible, *inter alia*, to determine what people 'need', rather than what they 'want'. See Hausman and McPherson, 1993, p. 706.

11   See also Waldron, 1995, p.19.

12   See, for example, Nozick, 1974, pp. 28-35.

13   For a discussion of the relationships among rights and utility, see Dworkin, 1978, pp. 94-96.

14   For more on the logical difficulties with rule-utilitarianism, see Scruton, 1994, pp. 282-283. See also Waldron, 1995, pp. 18-19.

15   See, for example Buchanan, 1994b, pp. 74-77.

16   For more on the Paretian liberal, see Sen, 1970, 1976, 1983. See also Gibbard, 1974; Deb, Pattanaik and Razzolini, 1997.

17   See, for example, Hausman and McPherson, 1993, esp. p. 716.

18   See, for example, Hausman and McPherson, 1993, p. 716.

19   A set of strategies is 'Nash' if no one can benefit by playing some other strategy, given others' strategies.

20   Professor Sen has himself criticized the notion of Pareto-improving strategies (1995, p. 14, fn 40). In any case, imperfect information and positive transaction costs militate against the structuring and enforcement of such contracts. See also Deb, Pattanaik and Razzolini, 1997.

21   Professor Dworkin has argued that 'external preferences' of any form present a problem for utilitarians. Given that external preferences 'for the assignment of goods and opportunities to others, or both' may be operative (1978, p. 234), and given that '[utilitarianism] owes much of its popularity to the assumption that it embodies the right of citizens to be treated as equals' (1978, p. 236), he concludes that 'utilitarians should not count external preferences of any form' (1978, p. 236). This, in Dworkin's view, applies with equal force to moralistic and altruistic external preferences (1978, p. 235). For a critical view of Dworkin's analysis, see Waldron, 1995, p. 17.

22   See also O'Neill, 1993, pp. 183-184; Dworkin, 1978, p. 94.

23   It is, of course, possible to question the notion of 'social preference'. See Buchanan, 1954a, 1954b, and the discussion in Chapter 7.

24   Rights- and goal-based moral theories may be distinguished as follows

>   The distinction between right-based and goal-based [moral] theories . . . is that a requirement is right-based if it is generated by a concern for some individual interest, goal-based if it is generated by a concern for something taken to be an interest of society as a whole (Waldron, 1995, p. 13).

See also, Dworkin, 1978, p. 172.

25   See also Almond, 1993, pp. 265-266; Goodin, 1993, p. 248; Dworkin, 1978, pp. 274-275; Waldron, 1995, pp. 18-19.

26   Some economists appear to have adopted the latter approach. The literature which suggests that corruption may be efficiency-enhancing is evidence of this. See, for example, Cheung, 1996; Tullock, 1996; Braguinsky, 1996; and Lui, 1996, for a discussion of the 'economics of corruption'--and of the role of corruption in improving allocative efficiency. Significantly,

> There is a strand in the corruption literature . . . suggesting that, in the context of pervasive and cumbersome regulations in developing countries, corruption may actually improve efficiency and help growth (Bardhan, 1997, p. 1322).

For a discussion of the role of consequentialism both in enhancing the 'possibility of unlimited corruption' and in producing "some interesting casuistry in 'applied ethics'" see Scruton, 1994, p. 283. See also Chapter 8, below.

27   See also Hausman and McPherson, 1993, p. 673.

6 The Implications for the Social Welfare Function

6.1 Introduction

To this point attention has largely centered on the indeterminacy of the Efficiency or Welfare Frontier. Manifestly, however, the logical, empirical and other problems adumbrated in earlier chapters have implications for the Social Welfare Function.

It is useful first to emphasize the intersection of SWT and what has come to be called Social Choice Theory (SCT). As Sen has emphasized, 'Social choice problems arise in aggregating the interests, preferences or judgements, or views, of different persons' (Sen, 1986, p. 214). Broadly speaking, SCT contemplates the aggregation of preferences or judgements for one of two purposes, namely, deciding and evaluating (Sen, 1995, p. 5). Insofar as SCT attempts a social evaluation of outcomes based on individual utility, it is, perforce, a branch of moral philosophy. For its part, the utilitarian Social Welfare Function may be understood to be an interest-aggregation mechanism which defines the optimal social outcome as the maximization of the sum of individual utilities. It is in this sense that the Social Welfare Function is understood to be a mechanism for deciding among states-of-affairs. Yet, because the Function is utilitarian, it presupposes the normative judgement that the desideratum, the standard of outcome evaluation, is that the best state is that which maximizes aggregate utility or 'welfare'.

It is understood, first, that fundamental questions have been raised about utilitarian and, therefore, consequentialist moral philosophy.[1] We have also seen (Chapter 5) that utilitarian moral philosophy is irreconcilable with the moral force of rights. And it is also clear that preference satisfaction may not be an adequate conception of individual and, *pari passu*, 'social' well-being. It is obvious, for example, that preferences may be based on false, idiosyncratic, highly contestable or malign beliefs. Indeed, it is possible to envision circumstances in which preferences should have to be "'laundered' before becoming suitable objects to be accorded moral weight" (Hausman and McPherson, 1993, p. 714). For present purposes, however, these issues are set aside. Interest centers instead on the implications for the Social Welfare

Function of the logical, empirical and other problems discussed in earlier chapters.

6.2 The Interpersonal Utility Comparison Problem, Again

The problem of interpersonal utility comparisons (IUCs) is familiar to most, if not all, economists. It seems clear, as well, that discussion of the problem has typically centered on utility comparability across persons. While this is not in dispute, there is another dimension to the problem. As the philosopher Robert E. Goodin has emphasized

> Aggregating individual utilities into some overall measure of social utility is an obviously tricky business, presupposing comparability of several sorts. It presupposes, first, comparability across goods . . . second, comparability across people . . . . (1993, p. 245).

While economists' interest has typically centered on the problem of utility comparability across people, little attention has been paid to the problem of comparability across goods. What seems generally not to be understood or acknowledged is that the 'across goods' problem is both extant and equally intractable.

Recall first that the discussion in Chapter 4 suggests, *inter alia*, that individual preference and value structures cannot meaningfully be captured by single-equation utility functions whose arguments are understood to be identical across individuals. Rather, each individual's multiple preference and value system requires representation by appeal to a multi-equation utility function, with each utility subfunction denoting a utility domain.[2] *Inter alia*, the multi-equation construct captures the notion of internal conflict; in particular, the intervention of moral appraisals on choice and other behavior. Emphasis was placed, moreover, on the endogeneity of preference and value structures. Thus, at a cross-section of time, the individual's preference and value structure reflects all manner of path-dependencies including learning, habits, cultural, and other intertemporal effects. When considered in the context of bounded rationality, information asymmetries, and positive transaction costs, the implication is clear: There can be no presumption that, at a cross-section of time, individuals will be possessed of identical multiple preference and value systems. It follows that, at a point in time, individual utility domains are not interpersonally comparable. Manifestly, this complicates the 'tricky business' of aggregating individual utilities. Yet, as Goodin suggests, there is also the problem of what he characterizes as 'comparability across goods'.

Whereas received neoclassical theory envisions a decision environment in which all individuals affect choices among the same goods, some fundamental features of observable suggest otherwise. As the discussion in Chapter 4 indicates, boundedly rational individuals confront an indefinitely large array of product types, with each product type typically appearing in differentiated forms. Given their subjective cognitive limitations and the intervention of positive transaction and decision costs, there can be no presumption that each individual will, at a cross-section of time, contemplate choice among the same subset of the available goods. In effect, the arguments of individuals' utility subfunctions will not, in any case of practical importance, be the same. This conclusion gains additional credence when it is appreciated that product types and their respective differentiates embody subjectively perceived technical, property rights and moral attributes. Reduced to its essentials, the problem envisioned here is that a world characterized by bounded rationality, information asymmetries, opportunistic behavior and positive transaction costs is, *pari passu*, a world in which objectively-defined and subjectively perceived decision environments diverge.

All of this has basic relevance to the IUC problem. Fundamentally, the IUC problem is complicated--at a cross-section of time--by the fact that individual preference and value domains are disparate, and by the fact that individuals affect choice among subjectively perceived subsets of the available goods. In short, in a decision environment characterized by bounded rationality--and all that it implies--the problem of IUCs across people and across goods appears to be irremediably complex.

There is, however, an additional dimension to the IUC problem. As has been emphasized, the received neoclassical theory and, *mutatis mutandis*, the new SWT assumes that the unboundedly rational individuals' preferences are both exogenously determined and intertemporally stable. Manifestly, this admittedly analytically convenient convention does not accord with reality. As the discussion in Chapter 4 suggests, path-dependencies are ubiquitous. The resulting endogeneity of preference and value structures reflects, *inter alia*, the interplay of learning, cultural effects, the emergence of new goods, public discourse, and the intervention of metapreferences; of preferences for preferences. This, in turn, suggests that 'policy' decisions are complicated by the fact that policies and institutions may affect the preferences which people form (Hausman and McPherson, 1993, p. 683).[3] More fundamentally, the endogeneity of preference and value structures implies that an intertemporal IUC problem obtains for the same individual (Furubotn, 1994, p. 34).

Whatever else is said, it is clear that these considerations militate against the specification of a meaningful Social Welfare Function. As Arrow has shown, absent IUCs,

> ... the only methods of passing from individual tastes to social preferences which will be satisfactory and which will be defined for a wide range of sets of individual orderings are either imposed or dictatorial (1951, p. 59).

This discussion has shown that, when allowance is made for fundamental features of objective reality, the complexity of the IUC problem is enhanced. A corollary of this is that Arrow's impossibility result retains its basic relevance. Such considerations have led Professor Sen to argue that '. . . the natural resolution of these problems lies in enriching the informational base . . .' (1995, p. 18). He has in mind such indicia of 'individual advantages' as 'real incomes, opportunities, primary goods, or capabilities' (Sen, 1995, p. 8).[4] While each of these proxies for IUCs is subject to difficulty, perhaps the most important conclusion is that 'normative social policy cannot be based solely on preferences' (Hausman and McPherson, 1993, p. 717). I shall return to this issue in Chapters 7 and 8.

6.3 Rights and 'Meddlesome' Preferences

The notion that 'normative social policy cannot be based solely on preferences' implicates the analysis proffered in Chapter 5. The discussion centered on the irreconcilability of SWT with another dimension of moral evaluation, rights. While the discussion underscored the point that utilitarian SWT cannot regard instrumentally important rights as having moral force--thereby undermining the path to Paretian optima or 'efficient' outcomes--the problem of respecting rights has basic relevance here. While the argument will not be replicated, the essential point is that, under certain conditions, *respect* for minimal personal liberties rules out the possibility of any social choice. All that is required for this result to obtain is that persons possess 'meddlesome preferences'; that they care about others' consumption patterns. As Professor Buchanan has argued (1994b, p. 75), such preferences are a palpable reality. Yet, if this is so, the efficacy of a Social Welfare Function as an interest-aggregation decision mechanism is called into question. In effect, the inability to affect IUCs and the impossibility of the Paretian liberal are to the Social Welfare Function what bounded rationality, information asymmetries, and positive transaction costs are to the Efficiency Frontier. An explicit accounting of observable features of objective reality renders both constructs indeterminate.

6.4 The Implications for the General Possibility Theorem

As is well known, Arrow's General Possibility Theorem establishes that, if IUCs are ruled out, there is no possible method of aggregating individual rankings of social alternatives which meets five apparently innocuous criteria (Arrow, 1951, pp. 24-31). Granting the logic of what has been said, the conclusion which emerges here is that the static and intertemporal IUC problems are intractable. Indeed, the problem is made manifestly more difficult if, as Professors Sen (1995, p. 18) and Buchanan (1994b, Chapter 3) suggest, preference and value formation should be informed by public discourse. This suggestion both acknowledges the endogeneity of preference and value structures and opens a Pandora's Box of problems. *Inter alia*, two particularly troublesome problems must be faced: (1) Which preferences and values should be promoted, and which institutions provide a framework within which desirable preferences will develop? (2) The potential conflict which may arise between first-order and metapreferences (Hausman and McPherson, 1993, p. 683). The upshot is that the malleability of preferences and values implicates both the Efficiency Frontier and the Social Welfare Function. With respect to the former, it is not clear 'how even to *define* an efficiency standard when individual preferences are malleable' (Frank, 1996, p. 119). With respect to the Social Welfare Function, the malleability of preference and value structures further animates the (intertemporal) IUC problem.

Finally, the inability of SWT to accommodate the moral force of rights underscores its inability to engage normative issues along any dimension of moral evaluation other than efficiency. Paradoxically, when, under plausible conditions, rights *are* respected, the role of the Social Welfare Function as an interest-aggregation decision mechanism is undermined.

6.5 Some Thoughts on the Idea of 'Social Preference'

To this point attention has centered on the empirical and logical difficulties which attend the construction and use of a utilitarian Social Welfare Function. There is, however, an even more fundamental, ontological problem.

As is well known, Professor Arrow (1951, p. 23) defined a Social Welfare Function as a functional relation that specifies a social ordering over all the social states for every set of individual preference orderings. It is possible, as Professor Buchanan long ago argued, to reject not only the transitivity of social preference, but the idea of social preference itself. In Buchanan's view, '. . . rationality or irrationality as an attribute of the social group implies the imputation to that group of an organic existence apart from that of its individual components' (Buchanan, 1954b, p. 116).

In view of Arrow's impossibility result, Professor Sen argues that Buchanan's objection is 'quite persuasive' when the idea of 'social preference' connotes the operation of social decision mechanisms such as voting procedures (Sen, 1995, p. 5). On the other hand, he concludes that, when the idea of 'social preference' is invoked in the context of social welfare judgements, Buchanan's objection has less force. In effect, Sen argues that, the impossibility result notwithstanding, when expressing a social judgement 'even an individual needs a concept (like social preference)'. For Sen, the concept of social preference is instrumentally important to the expression of social judgements; the expression of which is facilitated by the fact that, whereas IUCs are 'not an easy thing to do in social-decision mechanisms', they 'can be used by a person making social welfare judgement, or in agreed procedures for social judgements . . . .' (Sen, 1995, p. 9).

The essential point is that, insofar as attention centers on social decision mechanisms, Professor Buchanan's critique has unambiguous relevance. Arrow's impossibility result ensures that the idea of 'social preference' has no empirical counterpart. On the other hand, while it is possible to argue that, in principle, social judgements either implicitly or explicitly invoke the notion of 'social preference', some fundamental problems remain.

The threshold point is that the concept of social preference is instrumentally important to the new SWT. If one accepts the behavioral and technological postulates of the frictionless neoclassical decision environment, it is understood that a perfectly competitive system would be 'efficient' in the sense that the system would be impelled to a 'competitive' equilibrium somewhere along the Efficiency Frontier. Whether the competitive equilibrium represents an 'ethical' equilibrium depends on whether there is tangent at that point a social indifference curve (Furubotn, 1971). As we have seen, the presumption is that, if such a tangency does not obtain, a system of lump-sum taxes and bounties can be employed to secure the competitive-ethical equilibrium. In any case, the essential point is that, absent a single-valued, consistently-ordered, utilitarian Social Welfare Function, the only available standard of moral judgement is the efficiency standard; a standard which, in any case, is subject to empirical, logical and other difficulties. Yet, as Professor Sen has himself observed, '. . . Pareto efficiency can scarcely be an adequate condition for a good society' (Sen, 1995, p. 3).

Granting all of this, it is not clear how 'social preference', deployed in the context of SWT, can entertain the 'social judgements' to which Professor Sen refers. *Inter alia*, as we saw in Chapter 5, any attempt to embed rights in consequences or states-of-affairs must be unavailing. The desired antecedent rights cannot be derived from consequences. On the other hand, we have seen that utilitarian SWT cannot accommodate the moral force of rights and their correlative duties. And, finally, if minimal liberties over 'personal domains' *are* respected, the impossibility of the Paretian liberal militates against any social choice.

It seems clear that one important dimension of moral evaluation--of social judgement--rights, cannot be accommodated by SWT. This is troublesome for at least three reasons. First, the social welfare theorist and, *pari passu*, the 'user' of SWT is effectively disenfranchised. He cannot, meaningfully, deploy the theory to address questions related to the special force of rights. Second, the instrumental role in SWT of unattenuated exchange and property rights has been repeatedly emphasized. Yet, as we have seen, the social welfare theorist cannot regard these rights as having moral force. If one grants that 'rights have priority over considerations like utility or desert because they reflect the conditions under which it becomes possible for an agent to recognize and act on considerations like utility and desert' (Waldron, 1995, p. 19), this poses a considerable dilemma for social welfare theorists. Finally, if one regards justice as respect for rights,[5] this too poses a dilemma for social welfare theorists interested in articulating 'social judgements'.

The last point indirectly addresses another dimension of moral evaluation, justice. If the accommodation of rights poses an intractable problem for SWT, so too does justice. At the most rudimentary level, SWT is silent on the matter of justice. It is understood, for example, that initial resource endowments (which appear like 'manna from heaven') are important determinants, given the structure of relative prices and unattenuated exchange and property rights, of the point on the Efficiency Frontier to which the perfectly competitive system is impelled. Yet the theory is silent about the justice--however defined--of the initial endowments. Moreover, it is easy to show that, in the face of exogenously introduced technological change, SWT endorses a 'windfall ethic' (Furubotn, 1971).

There remains, of course, the question of the definition of justice. While this issue is more fully explored in Chapter 7, it is sufficient for present purposes to note that justice may be variously understood to consist in respect for rights (already addressed), mutual advantage or impartiality.[6] In the case of justice as mutual advantage, the social welfare theorist-qua-utilitarian confronts still another logical conundrum:

> The reconciliation between morality and self-interest that mutual advantage theorists seek is hard to achieve, since the presence of rules of justice creates a classic prisoner's dilemma: even if you and I jointly benefit from the rules, I will do still better if you obey them and I allow myself to violate them when it suits me (Hausman and McPherson, 1996, p. 159).

Suffice it to say that nothing in utilitarian SWT contemplates the moral force of rights and correlative duties. Utilitarian arguments can always be deployed in favor of not respecting rights and duties.

The view of justice as impartiality has found its most important contemporary articulation in the work of John Rawls (1971). While this view of justice will be more fully explored in Chapter 7, the essential point is that Rawls' first and second principles of justice (Rawls, 1971, p. 303) determine 'a framework of rights and institutions that will ensure maximal equal liberty and, insofar as is possible, fair equality of opportunity' (Hausman and McPherson, 1996, p. 156). Given that SWT is institutionless and irreconcilable with the moral force of rights, it is not clear that social welfare theorists are able, meaningfully, to engage this understanding of justice.

The upshot of all of this is that the concept of social preference to which Professor Buchanan objects is vulnerable on two levels. As Professor Sen concedes, the impossibility theorem militates against its use in the context of choices emerging from social decision mechanisms.[7] But, contrary to Sen's view, the notion of social preference--at least as it is deployed in SWT--has only limited use in moral or 'social welfare' judgements. Setting aside the empirical, logical and other difficulties outlined in earlier chapters, social welfare theorists can, in principle, conduct normative evaluation along one moral dimension, efficiency. Consideration of rights and justice must lie outside the purview of social welfare theorists.

6.6 The Implications for Consequence-Based Evaluation

As we have seen, the logical, empirical and structural problems which inhere in procedure-detached, consequence-based SWT are debilitating. It has been shown that an explicit accounting of fundamental features of observable reality renders both the Efficiency Frontier and the Social Welfare Function indeterminate. This, in turn, calls into question the efficiency standard, the only standard of normative appraisal to which the theory gives rise. Moreover, as we have seen, SWT is not accommodative of other dimensions of moral appraisal, notably rights and justice.

In the face of these difficulties, it seems appropriate that consideration be given to alternative approaches. The alternatives discussed in Chapter 7 take as their point of departure that consequence-based, procedurally-detached analysis is problematic. The first alternative, due to Professor Sen, seeks to integrate consequential and procedural considerations. The focus of the second approach is procedural or 'constitutional'. Styled the contractarian alternative, the approach has much in common with what has come to be called the New Institutional Economics. Roughly paraphrased, the objective is to 'get the institutions right'.

Notes

1   See, for example, Davis, 1993, pp. 205-218.
2   See Hausman and McPherson, 1993, p. 688; Aaron, 1994.
3   As Sen has observed, 'Social choice theory has tended to avoid this issue . . . .' (1995, p. 3). See also Chapters 7 and 8, below.
4   Broadly speaking, primary goods 'are things which it is supposed a rational man wants whatever else he wants' (Rawls, 1971, p. 92). The discussion in Chapter 7, below, distinguishes between primary natural and primary social goods. For more on 'the variety of methods which can be used in the attempt to give [interpersonal utility comparisons] a working basis', see Rothschild, 1993, pp. 91-96.
5   See, for example, Nozick, 1974, esp. pp. 150-153.
6   For a detailed discussion of alternative conceptions of justice, see Barry, 1989.
7   This conclusion is reinforced when it is recognized that "The impossibility result . . . can be extended and shown to hold even when the idea of 'social preference' is totally dropped and even when no conditions are imposed on 'internal consistency' of social choice" (Sen, 1995, p. 7).

7 Alternatives to Consequentialist Social Welfare Theory

7.1 Consequentialist Social Welfare Theory Debilitated: A Reprise

Much of the discussion to this point has centered on the theoretical foundations of the new SWT. While a replication of the argument would be both onerous and redundant, it is appropriate to highlight the major conclusions: (1) Once explicit account is taken of some fundamental features of observable reality, both the Efficiency Frontier and the Social Welfare Function are rendered indeterminate. (2) It has been shown that, even if one were to grant the existence of these fundamental constructs, the path to first-best Paretian optima is not secure. Whereas SWT implicitly assigns an instrumental role to unattenuated exchange and property rights, the duties correlative to these rights cannot, in utilitarian terms, have moral force. Moreover, when minimal personal liberties *are* respected, the impossibility of the Paretian liberal militates against any social choice. In short, SWT cannot accommodate any plausible rights construal. (3) Given the indeterminacy of the Efficiency Frontier and the Social Welfare Function, the only criterion for moral appraisal to which the theory gives rise--efficiency--is not operational. The point here is not that 'efficiency' in the sense of Pareto optimality is a controversial moral principle. It is. Rather, the point is that it cannot serve as a practical guide to public policy formulation.

7.2 The World As It Is

The root cause of these theoretical and ethical lacunae is social welfare theorists' commitment to outcomes-based, procedurally-detached analysis. Given that the underlying neoclassical theory is both intendedly value-free and institutionless, this comes as no surprise. The 'frictionless' neoclassical decision environment is, after all, characterized by unbounded rationality, by intertemporally stable, consistently-ordered and exogenously determined preference structures, by the absence of information asymmetries and, *pari passu*, by zero transaction costs. In such an environment decision costs are zero, and decision 'procedures' reduce to uncovering decision rules which are necessary (in a mathematical sense) to fully-informed, constrained optimization.

The problem with this stylized approach is not simply that it gives rise to the nirvana fallacy; to a failure to take account of unavoidable constraints. More fundamentally, the consequence-based, procedurally-detached approach ignores the basic relevance of ethically-motivated and other institutional side-constraints on action. At the most rudimentary level, the 'world as it is' is characterized by bounded rationality. The juxtaposition of this 'brute fact' against the growth of knowledge implies a growing competence difficulty gap, ubiquitous information asymmetries and, *pari passu*, opportunistic behavior. In such an environment, decision and, more generally, transaction costs can be minimized through the intervention of informal and formal side constraints. Yet, frictionless, intendedly value-free and institutionless SWT is unable even to address such issues. Because neither the behavioral and technical postulates nor the designed classes of implications of the underlying neoclassical theory contemplate institutional considerations, SWT cannot contemplate decisions at the constitutional level. In effect, the rules-of-the-game within which both private and public choices are affected fall outside the purview of SWT. This theoretical lacuna has many implications. *Inter alia*, the role and importance of ethical norms both in interpersonal relationships and in the increasingly impersonal market economy is implicitly denied. Equally important, all rights construals and conceptions of justice implicate 'rules-of-the-game'. It follows that important dimensions of moral evaluation are beyond the reach of received SWT.

Finally, whether in preference, welfare or rule-utilitarian form, SWT contemplates 'outcomes' defined in terms of utility. As we have seen, the problems which attend interpersonal utility comparisons are daunting, and likely irremediable. More fundamentally, the underlying preference and value structures may not be consistently-ordered, and are neither intertemporally stable nor exogenously determined. As we have seen, in the presence of unidentified, endogenously determined and, therefore, mutable preference and value structures, it is not clear how an efficiency standard might even be defined. The implications for the practical conduct of 'efficiency-driven' public policy are immediately clear (Furubotn, 1994, p. 35). Given that conse-quentialism and, *pari passu*, SWT is 'first and foremost, a standard for judging public action' (Goodin, 1993, p. 245), this is a formidable problem. Add to this the fact that one objective of public policy may be to change preference and value structures and the mutable preference problem becomes still more intractable (Sen, 1995, p. 16; Buchanan, 1994b, Chapter 3). The essential point is that what agents prefer--whether at a point in time or intertemporally--is unknowable. Moreover, it may be the case that some preferences--were they known--should have to be 'laundered' if they were to merit ethical approval. And, finally, the view that utility should be maximized is itself a complex--and controversial--moral judgement (Rawls, 1971, p. 91). *Inter alia*, the inter-vention of metapreferences raises an obvious question: Whose utility should be maximized? Add to this the intervention of false, idiosyncratic and contestable beliefs, cognitive dissonance and other palpable features of observable reality and it is not clear that the maximization of utility is consonant with the maximization of 'welfare'. Reduced to its essentials, the problem here is that '. . . identifying preference, choice and welfare begs too many important questions' (Hausman and McPherson, 1993, p. 688). Yet it is precisely these--and other--questions which SWT 'begs'. Included among these questions are dimensions of moral appraisal which are either irreconcilable with, or not contemplated by, SWT. Presumptively, people do care about 'well-being'. But they also care about freedom, rights, equality and justice (Hausman and McPherson, 1996, p. 119). Given the empirical, logical and other problems which inhere in SWT, we might plausibly wonder whether its consequence-based, procedurally-detached approach calls for fundamental revision. Indeed, given its inability meaningfully to contemplate alternative dimensions of moral evaluation, we might conclude, with Sugden, that 'Revealed preference welfarism . . . may have to be abandoned' (Sugden, 1993, p. 1961).

Whether one contemplates revising SWT or embracing an alternative, two approaches merit particular attention. The first, due to Professor Sen, retains a consequentialist focus, but incorporates some procedural considerations. The second, styled contractarian, has a procedural focus. I shall consider these approaches seriatim.

7.3 Sen's Consequentialist-Procedural Approach

Professor Sen's orientation is, in its fundamentals, consequentialist. He starts from a conception of what constitutes a 'good' life, and builds upon this foundation a theory of the social good. Insofar as he recognizes an obligation to promote good outcomes, his approach is consequentialist.[1] That said, Professor Sen's fundamental objection to consequentialist SWT is its 'informational poverty' (Klamer, 1989, p. 140).[2] On his view

> . . . there is no particular reason why [a] plurality of motivations cannot be accommodated within a social choice framework with more richly described social states and more articulated characterization of individual choices and behavior (Sen, 1995, p. 18).

While Sen is motivated, in part, by the force of Arrow's impossibility result and, in part, by the problems which attend interpersonal utility comparisons (Sen, 1995, p. 18), more is ultimately at issue

[Sen's] core argument is that the 'informational base' of welfarism is too thin to support an acceptable--and perhaps even a coherent--account of the social good. If we are to generate a theory of the social good, we must accept the relevance of information about features of the world other than individuals' revealed preferences (Sugden, 1993, p. 1947).

In the interest, *inter alia*, of enriching the informational base, Sen adopts two conventions. In his view, "living may be seen as consisting of a set of interrelated 'functionings', consisting of beings and doings" (Sen, 1992, p. 38). Thus, 'being adequately nourished' and 'being happy' are functionings. On this interpretation, there is no one-to-one correspondence between functionings and commodities. Whereas commodities may be instrumental to functionings (they may be used), the latter are an aspect of living. Granting this, a state of being is understood to consist in a vector of functionings, and an agent's choice among such vectors determines the kind of life he lives. Not all functioning vectors are, however, achievable. The set of feasible vectors for any agent is that person's capability set. In effect, the capability set determines the agent's opportunity to achieve well-being.[3]

While much can be said about this, it is clear that Sen's understanding of the notion of functionings is congruent with his emphasis on 'the plurality of our concerns' (Sen, 1992, p. 70). Indeed, his list of intrinsically valuable functionings includes 'being happy', 'having self-respect', 'being in good health', 'being adequately fed' and, significantly, 'acting freely' and 'being able to choose' (Sen, 1992, pp. 39, 51). While positive freedom[4] is therefore a dimension of well-being, it is not a functioning. Rather, it is identified with the capability set; with the set of feasible vectors of functionings (Sugden, 1993, p. 1951). On this interpretation, 'well-being is a function of both the capability set (representing the extent of positive freedom) and the chosen combination of functionings (representing dimensions of well-being other than positive freedom)' (Sugden, 1993, p. 1952).

The emphasis on positive freedom is congruent with Sen's view that 'The need to integrate procedural considerations in consequential analysis is especially important in the field of rights and liberties' (Sen, 1995, p. 13).[5] It is significant, however, that in setting out to combine the consequential and procedural approaches, Sen rejects the notion of preference-independent, consequence-detached rights (Sen, 1995, pp. 11-12 and 14). In rejecting the

Libertarian view of rights as absolute side constraints on action, Sen argues that 'perhaps the central question that is raised is the plausibility of making people's putative rights, in general, so dissociated from the effects of exercising them' (Sen, 1995, p. 14). On the logic that rights cannot be consequence-detached, Sen argues that consequential analysis can be employed in 'inverse form', *inter alia*, to determine which rights to protect. As we have seen, the problem with this approach is that ' . . . rights . . . have a normative life of their own, with implications that are neither reducible to, nor traceable by, direct considerations of utility' (Lyons, 1982, p. 133). Presumptively, while Sen's consequent states-of-affairs contemplate functionings rather than utility, the same prohibition applies: Desired consequences cannot be employed to determine which rights to protect.[6] Whether the rights which Sen seeks to protect are intrinsically valuable or merely instrumental, it is clear that he cannot derive them from desired consequences.

Whereas consequentialist SWT cannot accommodate any of the under-standings of justice, Sen's consequential-procedural approach contemplates a particular understanding of justice. In his view, capabilities provide the most appropriate informational base for a theory of justice. In effect, Sen's theory of justice demands equality of capabilities. Whereas contractarians like Rawls emphasize command over resources--in the sense of primary social goods--Sen emphasizes 'capabilities' and their correlative 'opportunities'.

The differences here require fuller explication. On Rawls' account, primary goods are 'things which it is supposed a rational man wants whatever else he wants' (Rawls, 1971, p. 92). He distinguishes, however, between primary natural and primary social goods. Primary natural goods are a 'person's natural endowments of characteristics that provide general means for achieving unspecified ends; examples include health, intelligence, and physical strength' (Sugden, 1993, p. 1955).[7] Whereas these primary natural goods are the property of the endowed agent, the income, wealth and authority which such goods are capable of generating are not his property (Rawls, 1971, pp. 14-15). Moreover, 'The natural distribution [of primary natural goods] is neither just nor unjust' (Rawls, 1971, p. 102). For their part, 'The primary social goods . . . are rights and liberties, opportunities and powers, income and wealth . . . . They are social goods in view of their connection with the basic structure; liberties and power are defined by the rules of major institutions and the distribution of income and wealth is regulated by them' (Rawls, 1971, p. 92).[8]

While he assigns lexical priority to rights (1971, p. 302), Rawls emphasizes that each of the primary social goods has the characteristic that 'With more of [them] men can generally be assured of greater success in carrying out their intentions and in advancing their ends, whatever these ends may be' (Rawls, 1971, p. 92). Given this understanding, Rawls' fundamental principle of justice is that primary social goods 'are to be distributed equally unless an unequal distribution of any, or all of [them] . . . is to everyone's advantage' (Rawls, 1971, p. 62). Then, given the 'framework of institutions required by equal liberty and fair equality of opportunity, the higher expectations of those better situated are just if and only if they work as part of a scheme which improves the expectations of the least advantaged. . . .' (Rawls, 1971, p. 75).

Insofar as the 'expectations' refer to 'advancing . . . ends, whatever these ends may be', Rawls' theory of justice starts with the presumption that resources--notably income and wealth, given the lexical priority of liberty--are to be distributed equally. Then, inequalities of resources--again, income and wealth--are justified if and only if, in the absence of these inequalities, those agents with least command over income and wealth would have had still less.

All of this has basic relevance to Sen's consequential-procedural approach. First, while Rawls assigns lexical priority to rights, Sen seeks to derive the rights 'to be protected' from desired outcomes. Second, while Rawls seeks to evaluate decision procedures--in particular, institutional arrangements[9]--Sen's primary focus is consequential. He seeks a substantive account of the 'good' or 'well-being' of the individual. Accordingly, his theory of justice is predicated on a demand for equality of capabilities: Insofar as capabilities constitute the feasible set of functionings (and a state of being is understood to consist in a vector of functionings), it is the equality of capabilities that matters to his consequentialist theory of justice. And herein lies the other fundamental difference between the two approaches. Whereas Rawls concentrates on 'resources'--again in the sense of income and wealth, given the lexical priority of rights--Sen argues that equal command over resources does not imply equal opportunities in the sense of functionings.[10] *Inter alia*, individuals differ in their ability to convert resources into functionings. On this account, it is better to base a theory of justice on capabilities, especially since resources do not have intrinsic value. Rather, their value is dependent upon the opportunities to which they give rise.

If one grants that resources like income and wealth do not have intrinsic value, and that it is the opportunities to which they give rise that 'count' for justice, then certain corollaries follow. First, whereas there is a metric by which income and wealth can be measured, Sen would deny that the value of these resources in terms of some numeraire reflects their intrinsic value. It follows that interpersonal comparisons of income and wealth have no meaning. This, in turn, renders the phrase 'equality of resources' vacuous. Second, if

Sen's 'equality of capabilities' approach is to be operational, a metric must exist by which to measure the intrinsic value of functionings and, ultimately, of capabilities. Given that Sen acknowledges that well-being is a 'broad and partly opaque concept' which is intrinsically ambiguous (Sen, 1992, pp. 46-49, 134), it is not clear how the necessary valuation process would proceed. In any case, if functionings have intrinsic value, information about individuals' preferences and choices is unavailing. Granting all of this, it is 'natural to ask how far Sen's framework is operational' (Sugden, 1993, p. 1953).

A number of problems attend Sen's attempt to integrate consequential and procedural analysis. First, he cannot logically derive the rights which he seeks to protect from the desired consequences. Second, it is not clear that a metric exists for the measurement of the theoretical concepts he employs. The notion of a vector of functionings may capture the idea of a state of being, while the notion of a feasible vector of functionings may, indeed, capture the idea of a person's capability set. But how are these notional concepts to be valued? Finally, Sen's project reduces, in its essentials, to developing a substantive account of the good or well-being of the individual. Given Sen's own appreciation of the intrinsic ambiguity of the concept of well-being, this is a daunting enterprise.

In the face of these difficulties, it seems clear that Professor Sen's consequentialist-procedural revision of received SWT may perhaps best be viewed as a powerful heuristic device. His approach highlights the need for an expansion of the 'informational base' of normative economics. Moreover, his approach opens the door for normative appraisal along other moral dimensions, notably rights and justice. And, finally, he explicitly introduces a procedural dimension which is notably absent in SWT.

Granting all of this, it is appropriate now to consider another alternative to SWT. The alternative advocated, *inter alia*, by James Buchanan, is procedural in orientation. Sen himself observes that

> [While] there are good reasons to doubt the adequacy of a purely procedural view (independent of consequences), just as there are serious defects in narrowly consequentialist views (independent of procedures),

the argument for a more procedural view of social decisions 'has much merit' (Sen, 1995, p. 18).

7.4 The Contractarian Alternative

The discussion of Professor Sen's consequentialist-procedural approach was motivated by two considerations. First, it is important in its own right. Second, the discussion facilitates consideration of the contractarian alternative.

The point of departure must be that, whereas SWT is consequentialist, and Professor Sen's approach seeks to integrate consequentialist and procedural modes of moral thought, the contractarian alternative is, in its essentials, procedural. Whether it is, or should be, consequence-detached is a matter to which we shall return below.

First, some preliminaries. It is recognized that every moral theory must answer two questions: (1) What are the demands that morality makes of persons, and (2) Why should persons feel obligated to respect these demands? As we have seen, a fundamental problem with consequentialist SWT is that it cannot accommodate the moral force of rights. Moreover, while Professor Sen's revision of the received SWT contemplates deriving rights from desired consequences, there are two, fundamental, problems. On the one hand, as we have seen, rights cannot be derived from consequences. On the other hand, even if this problem could be overcome, nothing in Professor Sen's consequentialist-procedural approach requires that consequentially-derived rights be respected. It seems clear, then, that neither SWT nor Sen's proffered revision of the traditional theory is accommodative of the obligation to respect rights, however they are construed.

What, then, may be said of the other dimension of moral evaluation, justice? Reduced to its essentials, neither SWT nor Sen's revision can accommodate the moral force of rules of justice, whatever they may be. In the case of the former, utilitarian arguments can always be deployed to overcome both rights and rules of justice. In the case of the latter, rights and rules of justice depend upon desired consequences. Yet the desired antecedents cannot be derived from desired consequences.

The two contemporary contractarian or social contract theories attempt, *inter alia*, to overcome these difficulties. The two theories differ, however, in fundamental ways. Whereas both theories accept the view that persons are, by nature, equals, the theory which regards justice as mutual advantage

> . . . stresses a natural equality of physical power, which makes it mutually advantageous for people to accept conventions that recognize and protect each other's interests and possessions (Kymlicka, 1993, p. 188).

For its part, the theory which regards justice as impartiality

... stresses a natural equality of moral status, which makes each person's interests a matter of common or impartial concern (Kymlicka, 1993, p. 188).

Given that the two theories represent contemporary--and competing--contractarian views, we shall evaluate both.

Justice as Mutual Advantage

The point of departure of the mutual advantage approach is that, while there is nothing inherently right or wrong about either the goals which persons pursue or the means employed to pursue them, it is mutually advantageous for persons to adopt conventions against harming each other (Kymlicka, 1993, p. 189). On this account, the bargaining by which these conventions are adopted is the *process* by which a community establishes its 'social contract'. The conventions which constitute the 'social contract' are seen as providing a moral code; a code which is 'generated as a rational constraint from the non-moral premises of rational choice' (Gauthier, 1986, p. 4).

Both because no account is taken of which goals are pursued, and because there is no presumption that particular goals ought to be promoted, the theory is not consequentialist. Rather, the theory is procedural in orientation, with the process of convention adoption contemplating bargaining among rational, self-interested agents. In effect, the obligation to respect the conventions adopted is grounded in the idea that bargaining proceeds 'among expected utility maximizers with common knowledge of everyone's capabilities, endowments, and preferences' (Hausman and McPherson, 1996, p. 158). Given this rich informational base, the presumption is that a rational agent will not agree to accept less than he could get in the absence of agreement. To the extent that agents possess heterogeneous capabilities, this bargaining constraint will result in the emergence of asymmetric gains. Moreover, the presumption is that the process of cooperation will itself yield gains. Whereas a just society would preserve the inequalities in gains that accrue as a result of prior advantages, the gains from cooperation would be distributed in accordance with a principle of 'minimax relative concession'. In effect, 'the largest concession anyone would have to make should be as small as possible' (Hausman and McPherson, 1996, p. 159).

Given the argument developed in earlier chapters, serious questions attach to the 'original position' contemplated by the theory. The notion that bargaining agents are possessed of full knowledge of everyone's capabilities, endowments and preferences is impossible to reconcile with a world characterized by bounded rationality. Moreover, it is clear that bargaining among narrowly self-interested agents who, by the nature of the theory, must be presumed to be inclined toward opportunistic behavior implies *ex ante* and *ex post* transaction costs; costs of which the theory takes no explicit account. Yet, even if these fundamental objections were set aside, the problem of respecting the adopted principles of justice is daunting. Given that goals and the means of achieving them are neither right nor wrong, and given that agents are narrowly self-interested, nothing in the theory assures a commitment to obey the rules of justice: Even if two agents, A and B, jointly benefit from the rules, A can do better if B obeys the rules, and A allows himself to violate the rules whenever it suits him. While Gauthier (1986) argues that, in the face of this prisoner's dilemma, it may be in B's self-interest to cultivate the kind of character in A that will lead A to obey the rules of justice, this leads to still other problems. *Inter alia*, the implicit suggestion that preferences and values are endogenously determined and mutable further erodes the plausibility of the informational base contemplated by the original position.

Finally, if there is nothing in the theory which implies respect for the adopted rules of justice, the same may be said of rights. The presumption is that bargaining among rational, self-interested agents possessed of asymmetric capabilities will result in the emergence of conventions which accord rights to various agents. Yet, because the 'mutual advantage' form of contractarianism 'does not view individuals as having any inherent moral rights or status' (Kymlicka, 1993, p. 189), the theory cannot accommodate the moral force of rights. In effect, the theory does not contemplate a moral obligation to respect the rights accorded by the adopted conventions. The problem here is similar to the conundrum which confronts social welfare theorists. Recall that social welfare theorists cannot regard the rights which are instrumentally important to the achievement of first-best Paretian optima as having moral force. However, whereas the latter problem arises because SWT is a hybrid moral theory,[11] the 'rights' problem arises for mutual advantage theorists because

> . . . rights flow from the constraints necessary for mutually beneficial co-operation, even when the activity in which people co-operate is the exploitation of other individuals (Kymlicka, 1993, p. 190).

Reduced to its essentials, the view of justice as mutual advantage is encumbered by a number of empirical and logical difficulties. On the one hand, the rich informational base contemplated by the original position is difficult to reconcile with definable features of observable reality; in particular, with bounded rationality and positive transaction costs. On the other hand, the theory's proponents cannot resolve the 'commitment' problem without appeal to the notion that appropriate values may have to be 'cultivated'. The problem here is not simply that the presumed mutability of preferences and values is difficult to reconcile with the presumption that bargaining agents are fully-informed about others' preferences, endowments and capabilities. More funda-mentally, one might plausibly ask, How are these values--respect for the agreed upon rules of justice and rights--to be 'cultivated' if agents are presumed to be narrowly self-interested, expected utility maximizers? Yet, even if these problems were soluble, a core problem would remain: Nothing in the mutual advantage approach contemplates moral claims which are *prior* to the pursuit of mutual advantage. If one accepts the view that there are such prior moral claims, then the theory of justice as mutual advantage will be unacceptable. This is the perspective of the proponents of a theory of justice as impartiality.[12]

Justice as Impartiality

The theory of justice as impartiality is grounded in Kant's Categorical Imperative. While the latter is formulated in a number of ways, the version of immediate interest is the 'Formula of the End in Itself' which 'demands that we treat humanity in your own person or in the person of any other never simply as a means but always at the same time as an end' (O'Neill, 1993, p. 178). On this account--and other formulations of the Categorical Imperative--one must seek to act on principles that all others could share, and on principles that 'respect all others' capacities to act' (O'Neill, 1993, p. 179). Principles of justice, then, are those principles which must be adopted if persons are to be treated as ends rather than as means to ends. They are, moreover, principles which are universalizable for rational beings (O'Neill, 1993, p. 179). Finally, respect for others' capacities to act demands that rights and their correlative duties be respected.

Proponents of the view of justice as impartiality take the prior commit-ment to the moral equivalence of persons as given. From this Kantian perspective, justice demands the promotion of institutions--in the sense of principles or rules of the game--which respect the *moral* equivalence of persons. On this account, the social contracts which give rise to these institutions do not justify the view of persons as ends in themselves. This is simply assumed. Rather, in contrast to the mutual advantage approach, the contract device is used to negate--rather than to reflect--unequal bargaining power. With this in mind, John Rawls, the best-known proponent of the view of justice as impartiality argues that a contract can give equal consideration to each of the contractors--but only if the original position contemplates negotiation from a position of equality. It follows that, in the original position, the principles which shape a just society must be chosen behind a 'veil of ignorance' which deprives each negotiator of knowledge of the role he would occupy in that society (Rawls, 1971, p. 12). Then, behind the veil of ignorance,

> The parties regard moral personality and not the capacity for pleasure and pain as the fundamental aspect of the self. They do not know what final aims persons have, and all dominant-end conceptions are rejected. . . . The parties' aim in the original position is to establish just and favorable conditions for each to fashion his own unity. Their fundamental interest in liberty and in the means to make fair use of it is the expression of their seeing themselves as primarily moral persons with an equal right to choose their mode of life. Thus they acknowledge the two principles of justice to be ranked in serial order as circumstances permit (Rawls, 1971, p. 563).

This formulation is clearly not consequentialist, either in the sense of utilitarian SWT, or in the sense of the consequentialist-procedural approach employed by Sen. Indeed, the parties behind the veil of ignorance do not know each others' 'final aims'. The parties, do however, regard moral personality as the fundamental aspect of self, and they do give lexical priority to liberty. Indeed, the 'two principles of justice for institutions' are:

> *First Principle*: Each person is to have an equal right to the most extensive total system of equal basic liberties compatible with a similar liberty for all.
> *Second Principle*: Social and economic inequalities are to be arranged so that they are both:
>   (a)   to the greatest benefit of the least advantaged, . . . , and
>   (b)   attached to offices and positions open to all under conditions of fair equality of opportunity (Rawls, 1971, p. 302).

While he acknowledges that its 'drawback . . . is that it lacks the definite structure of the two principles in serial order', Rawls proffers a General Conception of justice:

> All social primary goods--liberty and opportunity, income and wealth, and the bases of self-respect--are to be distributed equally unless an unequal distribution of any or all of these goods is to the advantage of the least favored (Rawls, 1971, p. 303).[13]

As we saw in section 7.3, above, emphasis is placed on the impartial--and, therefore, equal--distribution of primary social goods. The distribution of primary natural goods--'such as health and vigor, intelligence and imagination'

(Rawls, 1971, p. 62)--is 'neither just nor unjust' (Rawls, 1971, p. 102). In any case, the essential point is that the notion which animates the duty to promote just or impartial institutions is Kantian. The duty does not derive from consent or mutual advantage. Rather, the duty to promote impartial institutions is 'simply owed to persons as such' (Kymlicka, 1993, p. 191). Granting this, the content of persons' natural duty of justice is embodied in "a basic principle of impartial deliberation--i.e., that each person take into account the needs of others 'as free and equal beings'" (Kymlicka, 1993, p. 191).

A central issue is, of course, whether one is willing to accept the prior commitment which underlies the theory. As has been emphasized, the theory of justice as impartiality can neither defend nor generate the Kantian idea that persons matter in and of themselves. Rather, the theory presupposes this basic moral judgement. It follows that

> The ultimate evaluation of Kantian contractarianism depends, therefore, on one's commitment to the ideals of moral equality and natural duty that underlie it (Kymlicka, 1993, p. 194).

Whatever else is said, it seems clear that most economists--including social welfare theorists--embrace a prior commitment to value choice, self-determination, agency and independence.[14] Granting this, economists may not be predisposed to reject the Kantian view of persons as free and equal beings. Indeed, it is possible to argue that

> This belief is found not only in Kantian ethics, but throughout the ethical tradition of the West, both Christian (we are all God's children), and secular (utilitarianism provides its own non-contractual interpretation of the requirement for equal consideration of persons. . . .) (Kymlicka, 1993, pp. 192-193).[15]

Yet, whether or not others find this argument persuasive, I share the view that

> While the idea of contracting from an original position cannot justify our basic moral judgements, since it presupposes them, it does serve some useful purposes. It can render our judgements more determinate (contractual agreements must be explicitly and publicly formulated), render them more vivid (the veil of ignorance is a vivid way of expressing the moral requirement of putting ourselves in other people's shoes), and can dramatize our commitment to them (the veil of ignorance dramatizes the claim that we would accept a certain principle however it affected us). In these and other ways, the contract device illuminates the basic ideas of morality as impartiality, even if it cannot help defend those ideas (Kymlicka, 1993, p. 193).

These 'practical' considerations are, in my view, important in their own right. As we shall see in Chapter 8, they have basic relevance when attention centers on what might be characterized as the public policy process.

There are, of course, other objections to the view of justice as impartiality. Economists, in particular, have been skeptical about Rawls' difference principle; of the notion that society should maximize the primary social goods or 'resources' of the least advantaged. Two responses to this objection seem particularly appropriate. First, behind the veil of ignorance it is rational to seek to minimize the potential costs of being among the least advantaged. Second, as has been emphasized, Rawls' understanding of primary social goods contemplates 'rights and liberties, powers and opportunities, income and wealth' (Rawls, 1971, p. 62). Given the lexical priority assigned to rights, the application of Rawls' two principles of justice may be read as determining a framework of rights and institutions 'that will insure maximal equal liberty and, insofar as it is possible, fair equality of opportunity' (Hausman and McPherson, 1996, p. 156). Arguably, these principles are reconcilable with most economists' commitment to value choice, self-determination, agency and independence. In any case, one might argue that economists have focused excessively on what they take to be the redistributive implications of Rawls' approach:

> Rawls' views should lead economists instead to think about the design of institutions that will minimize the need for redistribution efforts, and it should lead them to focus on the means out of which individuals construct their own goods rather than directly on satisfying preferences (Hausman and McPherson, 1996, p. 157).

Given the institutional vacuum which both characterizes and encumbers the new SWT, this appears to be sage advice. And, given what has been said in earlier chapters about the unidentified nature of agents' endogenously determined preferences and values, an outcomes-based, procedurally-detached approach is clearly problematic.[16]

Granting the logic of what has been said, I am persuaded that economists' attention should center on the variant of contractarian analysis which regards justice as impartiality. The approach has much to commend it. *Inter alia*, unlike the received SWT, it is not reliant upon theoretical constructs which have no operational counterpart. Moreover, it is accommodative of dimensions of moral appraisal--notably, rights and justice--which SWT cannot, logically, reach. And, finally, the approach has practical implications for the construction of political institutions.

The view that the contractarian approach employed by Rawls deserves the attention of economists is shared by others. I have in mind, in particular, the work of Nobel laureate James Buchanan.

An Economist's Perspective

James Buchanan is widely acknowledged as a founder of the field of public choice or the new political economy. What is perhaps less widely appreciated is his emphasis on the need for a procedural or constitutional approach to economics; an approach which takes explicit account of what he styles economics' 'ethical moorings'.

The basic thrust of Buchanan's objections to the new SWT has been outlined in earlier chapters. *Inter alia*, he objects to the deployment of a Social Welfare Function as a mechanism of social decision and, more generally, to the idea of 'social preference'. Reduced to its essentials, his argument is animated by a rejection of the imputation of an organic existence to 'society' which is independent of a society's constituent members.[17] And, while he rejects the Bergson-Samuelson Social Welfare Function, Professor Buchanan is equally clear about the problems which attend the specification of the Efficiency Frontier. *Inter alia*, the endogeneity and unidentified nature of preference and value structures militate against the specification of the Frontier.[18] Indeed, on his view, the intersection of metapreferences and of the role and importance of moral rules in economic settings[19] underscores the importance of 'preaching'; of, *inter alia*, deliberate, systematic investment in the 'institutions of socialization and acculturization' (Buchanan, 1994b, p. 74).[20] That this suggestion is reminiscent of the Adam Smith of *The Theory of Moral Sentiments* is itself significant. But more important for present purposes is the corollary: The mutability of preference and value structures both renders the Efficiency Frontier indeterminate and further animates the interpersonal utility comparison problem. These and other considerations have led Professor Buchanan to suggest that

> Economists should cease proffering policy advice as if they were employed by a benevolent despot, and they should look to the structure within which political decisions are made (Buchanan, 1987, p. 243).

This passage is revealing in a number of respects. First, the reference to a 'despot' appears to be motivated by Arrow's impossibility result. Second, the invocation of the notion of a 'benevolent' despot is evocative of the idea that economists engaged in the provision of 'policy advice' do not take sufficient account of the self-interest of politician-agents. On this interpretation,

> The people or the constitutional assembly are the principals and politicians or bureaucrats are the agents. The contract between them should be set up in such a way that the agents are motivated to act in the interests of the principal (Sandmo, 1990, p. 61).

In effect, whereas consequence-based, procedurally-detached SWT implicitly assumes that public sector agents behave in a manner consonant with the attainment of Pareto-optimal and/or ethical equilibria,[21] Buchanan regards this presumption to be politically naive. For the assumption to have empirical content, the analyst should have to assume either that public sector agents are motivated to act in this way, or that principals could perfectly monitor their agents' behavior. On Professor Buchanan's view--a view which I share--neither assumption is plausible.[22] What is required, then, is a system of constitutional constraints; constraints which, in turn, would be established behind a 'veil of uncertainty'. The latter may be understood to be the constitutional economists' analogue for the Rawlsian 'veil of ignorance'.

Whereas the focus of consequentialist SWT is on 'outcomes', the 'Constitutional economics [research program] directs analytical attention to the *choice among constraints*' (Buchanan, 1991, p. 5). Interest centers, then, upon endogenously generated constraints, including ethical norms. Thus

> . . . we should recognize that the efficacy of any market order depends critically on the endogenous behavioral constraints that are in existence, and, further, that, to an extent, these constraints may themselves, be 'constructed' (Buchanan, 1994a, p. 125).

Buchanan's central idea is that these endogenous behavioral constraints can be regarded as emerging from a rational calculus (Buchanan, 1994a, p. 128); that it is in everyone's interest to step behind the veil of uncertainty and, impartially, to construct rules of the game whose 'publicness' embodies the prospect of positive expected gains by all parties.[23] Whereas 'conflictual' or 'ordinary' politics may imply 'winners' and 'losers',

> participation in the inclusive political game that defines the rules for ordinary politics may embody positively valued prospects for all members of the polity (Buchanan, 1991, p. 10).[24]

While it is clear that the motives which animate the move behind the 'veil of uncertainty' are more self-interested than those contemplated by Rawls, the 'hard core' of the constitutional economics paradigm is, distinctly, Kantian/ Rawlsian:

> All individuals must be presumed capable of making rational choices among alternatives in accordance with individually autonomous value-scales. And this generalization does not allow derivation of collective action whether or not directed toward choices among constraints, from individual evaluations on anything other than an equal weighting. To introduce a weighting scheme through which the evaluation of some persons in the community are deemed more important than other persons would require resort to some supra-individualistic source which is, of course, ruled out by adherence to the individualistic postulate. In this sense, the whole of the constitutional economics research program rests squarely on a democratic foundation (Buchanan, 1991, p. 16).

In short, while the 'hard core' of constitutional economics contemplates the 'foundational position' of methodological individualism and the postulate of rational choice (Buchanan 1991, pp. 14-15), it also demands respect for persons as autonomous, choosing agents. The link to the Kantian/Rawlsian contractarian approach is therefore clear. The link is further strengthened by the emphasis on fairness or impartiality:

> . . . the legitimacy of basic constitutional principles is judged not against some predefined 'ideal system' but in terms of the process from which these principles emerge. The normative focus is on the characteristics of the process of constitutional choice, not on characteristics of choice-outcomes as such. Furthermore, . . . a 'good' or 'proper' process is defined as one that assures *fairness* or *impartiality* in the rules that emerge (Buchanan, 1991, p. 59).

Finally, while Rawls' theory of justice as impartiality accords lexical priority to rights, Buchanan, effectively, does the same:

> . . . it is the voluntariness of choice that, from a contractarian perspective, constitutes the essential prerequisite of fairness (Buchanan, 1991, p. 59).

In sum, as Buchanan himself acknowledges, his approach 'has affinities with the familiar construction of John Rawls (1971)' (Buchanan, 1987, p. 249). Whereas, on Buchanan's account, the two approaches differ in that Rawls employs the veil of ignorance and the fairness criterion 'to derive principles of justice that emerge from a conceptual agreement at a stage prior to the selection of a political constitution' (Buchanan, 1987, p. 249), the two enterprises clearly have much in common. As we have seen, while both eschew the efficiency concept (in the sense of Paretian optimality) and outcomes-based evaluation generally, both accord lexical priority to rights, and both regard justice as impartiality.[25] Finally, while Rawls' second principle of justice contemplates-- subject to the lexical priority of rights--an equal distribution of primary social goods, Buchanan suggests that

> Behind a sufficiently thick veil of uncertainty and/or ignorance, contractual agreement on rules that allow for some in-period transfers seems clearly to be possible (Buchanan, 1987, p. 249).

That said, it is clear that, whereas Rawls envisions 'rational legislators suitably constrained by the veil of ignorance. . . . [As] Ideal legislators [who] do not vote their interests' (1971, p. 284), Buchanan argues that voter-principals would not, at the constitutional stage, want to leave redistribution to the discretion of their self-interested politician-agents. On this logic,

> If [principals at the constitutional stage] favor measures to equalize resources, they would prefer to embed particular distributive rules, say a negative income tax financed by a flat rate tax directly into the constitution. Such constitutional distri- butive rules (like the institutions mandated by Rawls' principles of justice) should not in fact be considered redistributive since they would figure into the underlying definition of property rights. . . . (Hausman and McPherson, 1996, p. 160).[26]

While Buchanan acknowledges that the 'precise features of a constitu- tionally approved transfer structure' are indeterminate 'because of the restriction of evaluative judgement to the process of constitutional agreement' (Buchanan, 1987, p. 249), this much can be said: '[Buchanan] does advocate a concept of justice as fairness with the important condition for fairness being equality of starting points' (Sandmo, 1990, p. 62). Presumptively, Buchanan's approach does not contemplate equality of starting points in the sense of equality of primary natural goods. As we have seen, the distribution of such goods--notably 'natural talents and the contingencies of social circumstance'--is neither just nor unjust (Rawls, 1971, p. 102). Rather, the presumption must be that Buchanan has in mind equality of opportunity. While, as Hausman and McPherson have observed, equal opportunity is a 'somewhat vague notion' (1993, p. 697), Buchanan does not regard this indeterminancy as a debility. On his account,

. . . the origins of the rules that are in existence at any particular time and in any particular polity cannot satisfactorily be explained by the contractarian model. The purpose of the contractarian exercise is not explanatory in this sense. It is, by contrast, justificatory in that it offers a basis for normative evaluation (Buchanan, 1987, p. 249).

At issue, in other words, are not the specifics of any particular transfer or other program. What is at issue is the impartiality of the *process* which generated the rules of the game. Granting this,

Normatively, the task for the constitutional political economist is to assist individuals, as citizens who ultimately control their own social order in their continuing search for those rules of the political game that will best serve their purposes, whatever these might be (Buchanan, 1987, p. 250).

It is these maxims which inform the discussion in the next chapter.

Notes

1   See also Sen, 1995, pp. 7-8.
2   See also Pettit, 1993, pp. 231 and 241.
3   For a discussion of the role of 'opportunities' in consequentialist theory, see Pettit, 1993, p. 232.
4   For a taxononomy of positive, negative, and other rights, see Almond, 1993, p. 259.
5   On his view, "the violation or fulfillment of basic liberties and rights tends to be ignored in traditional utilitarian welfare economics, not just because of its consequentialist focus, but particularly because of its 'welfarism', whereby consequent states of affairs are judged exclusively by the utilities generated in the respective states" (Sen, 1995, p. 13). See also Chapter 5, above.
6   See also Chapter 5.
7   See also Rawls, 1971, p. 62.
8   Like Adam Smith, Rawls also regards a 'sense of one's worth' as a 'very important primary good'. For a discussion of Smith's view of the role and importance of the 'desire for approbation', see Muller, 1993, pp. 51-54.
9   In particular, he seeks a system of fair rules within which individuals with disparate--and unknown--ends can cooperate to their mutual advantage (Sugden, 1993, p. 1957).
10   *Inter alia*, persons are endowed with differing primary natural goods.
11   See the discussion in Chapter 5, above.
12   For an additional critical appraisal of the theory of justice as mutual advantage, see Buchanan, 1991, Chapter 16.
13   Again, the emphasis on self-respect is reminiscent of Adam Smith's view. See footnote 8.
14   See section 5.2, above.

15   In the case of utilitarian SWT, the essential idea is that the maximization of the sum of individual utilities ought to be promoted, regardless of the content of individual preferences.

16   A final objection to Rawls' approach has already been discussed. See section 7.3, above, for a discussion of Professor Sen's view that normative analysis should contemplate functionings and capabilities rather than primary social goods or resources.

17   As we have seen, this objection is independent of Arrow's impossibility result; a result whose importance for social decision processes Buchanan acknowledges.

18   See, for example, Sandmo, 1990, pp. 55 and 57.

19   See, for example, Buchanan, 1994a, p. 124.

20   Buchanan emphasizes that, because there will always be persons who behave opportunistically, 'formal laws become necessary'. But he argues, "the 'laws and institutions' should always be considered to be supplementary to and complementary with the operative set of moral rules that prompt persons to constrain their own choice behavior" (1994a, p. 133).

21   As has been suggested, an 'ethical' equilibrium contemplates a tangency of a social indifference curve and the Efficiency Frontier (Furubotn, 1971).

22   See, for example, Buchanan, 1986, pp. 254-255.

23   See also Buchanan, 1987, p. 246.

24   See also Hausman and McPherson, 1996, p. 160.

25   Buchanan's understanding of 'efficiency' relates to procedures and constitutions rather than to outcomes. As Sandmo has observed,

> Buchanan's ideas about efficiency are not the same as the ones current in neoclassical welfare economics. He argues that because preferences and costs are unobservable, efficiency must be judged by the processes through which transactions are carried out, not by the results (1990, p. 57).

26   Interestingly, Rawls argues that, 'since the burden of taxation is to be justly shared . . . . a proportional expenditure tax may be part of the best tax scheme' (Rawls, 1971, p. 278).

8 Contractarian Analysis and Political Institutions

8.1 The Sterility of Consequentialist Social Welfare Theory

The point of departure of this, the final chapter, is the recurring theme of this book: Because of the logical, empirical and other difficulties associated with the underlying, neoclassical theory, the fundamental constructs of the new SWT are indeterminate. Moreover, consequentialist, utilitarian SWT is neither reconcilable with the moral force of rights and their correlative duties nor accommodative of construals of justice which emphasize rights or impartiality.[1] Finally, because it is both institutionless and intendedly value-free, SWT cannot meaningfully be deployed for the purpose of institutional evaluation. Indeed, the only evaluative standard to which the theory gives rise, efficiency, is outcomes, rather than procedurally-based. Thus, even if one were to grant the existence of the Efficiency Frontier and, at the same time, to assume that instrumentally important rights would be respected, the procedural aspects of the path to first-best Paretian optima fall outside the purview of the theory. Precisely because it is both intendedly value-free and procedurally-detached, SWT is incapable of addressing the subject matter of constitutional--or contractarian--political economy.[2] The focus of the latter, as we have seen, is the normative appraisal of alternative institutional designs. Central to the evaluation process are, of course, the dimensions of normative appraisal with which SWT is either irreconcilable or non-accommodative.

Before attention shifts to the question of institutional design, it is important, first, to contemplate some of the unintended consequences of reliance upon the efficiency standard.

8.2 Efficiency and the Growth of Government

It is at least arguable that the nirvana fallacy to which I have repeatedly referred has led some economists to draw conclusions which may not follow, given the objective features of reality. *Inter alia*, strict adherence to the notion that violations of one or more of the marginal equivalences associated with Pareto optima implies market failure has caused some economists to conclude that, necessarily, the government can do better:

> In their analyses of the effects of externalities welfare economists may sometimes have fallen into the trap of arguing that if the market fails, the government is sure to do better. . . . thereby making welfare economics and its applications much more progovernment and prointerference than could be justified on scientific grounds (Sandmo, 1990, p. 58).

On Sandmo's account, the propensity of some social welfare theorists implicitly or explicitly to assume that 'the government is sure to do better' may be attributable to their failure to appreciate that SWT is not a 'positive theory of government'. Yet

> . . . to recommend public action to correct for market failure requires a positive theory of government behavior to convince us that there is in fact reason to expect that the government will do better than the market. Sometimes, no doubt, it will do worse (Sandmo, 1990, p. 59).

Sandmo's generic point is well taken. But there is, ultimately, more at issue. If one grants the logic developed in earlier chapters, it seems appropriate to conclude that 'the Pareto criterion is not a device that can be employed meaningfully in assessing economic policy' (Furubotn, 1994, p. 35). The essential point is that, in a world of 'frictions'--*inter alia*, of bounded rationality and positive transaction costs--the marginal conditions for a Pareto optimum no longer have basic relevance. Yet, even if the notion of a 'frictionless' system were accepted, we should have to acknowledge that

> . . . we still know very little about the benefits and costs of antitrust, banking and security regulation, and regulation aimed at protecting consumers from fraud. We know very little about the dynamic impacts of regulation on innovation, investment and productivity. We know little about designing political institutions that promote more efficient regulation (Hahn, 1998, p. 209).

If Sandmo is right, and social welfare theorists may, indeed, fall into the trap of arguing that 'if the market fails, the government is sure to do better', then these empirical lacunae should give economists pause. In any case, it is somewhat anomalous that a theory grounded in choice, self-determination, agency, independence and the notion of a minimalist state[3] should be employed to rationalize all manner of 'Pareto improving' government interventions. Perhaps the fundamental problem is captured by Stiglitz' invocation of SWT:

As a long-time student of the public sector, I welcomed the opportunity to come to Washington as a member of the Council of Economic Advisers and later to become the Chairman of the Council. . . .

To be sure, I came as an activist . . . with a view about what it was that government should, and should not be doing. My reference point was the fundamental theorems of welfare economics. . . . it has been shown that in the presence of imperfect information or incomplete markets, the economy will not be Pareto efficient; in other words, there will always be some intervention by which the government can make everyone better off. . . . (Stiglitz, 1998, pp. 3-4).[4]

Given the problems which attend the specification of, and the path to, the Efficiency Frontier,[5] this is a remarkable perspective. To the extent that it is representative of the views of other economist-qua-policy advisers, it should come as no surprise that SWT has been employed to underwrite the expansion of government.

8.3 Efficiency and Corruption

If appeals to the efficiency standard may have sometimes resulted in a 'progovernment and prointerference' posture beyond that which 'could be justified on scientific grounds', it also has been employed in other, presumably unintended, ways. As we saw in section 5.3, above, social welfare theorists must either argue that the rights which they regard as instrumentally important are morally exigent in themselves (and reject the efficiency standard), or embrace the efficiency standard and deny the moral force of rights. Arguably, the literature which suggests that corruption may be efficiency-enhancing suggests that some economists may have adopted the latter approach. Lui has suggested, for example, that 'corruption is an optimal response to market distortions and may improve allocative efficiency' (1996, p. 26). For his part, Gordon Tullock has argued that 'Most people who object to corruption probably do so on moral grounds without considering the practical effects' (1996, p. 7). Yet, on Tullock's view, this is, presumably, to miss the point:

. . . corruption . . . may have some redeeming features. It may make possible smaller or no salary payments to [government] officials who, if carefully supervised, will still carry out their functions on a fee-for-service basis (1996, p. 6).[6]

The suggestion that corruption among government officials 'may have some redeeming features' is both remarkable and, obviously, irreconcilable with the view of justice as impartiality. But if Tullock's point relates specifically to the behavior of government officials, Serguey Braguinsky makes a generic point:

> The literature has pointed out that some forms of corruption are more detrimental to growth, while others can be considered even beneficial, given the underlying regulation (1996, p. 14).

The literature to which Braguinsky refers has been summarized as follows:

> There is a strand in the corruption literature . . . suggesting that, in the context of pervasive and cumbersome regulations in developing countries, corruption may actually improve efficiency and help growth. Economists have shown that, in the second-best world when there are pre-existing policy induced distortions, additional distortions in the form of black-marketeering, smuggling, etc., may actually improve welfare even when some resources have to be spent in such activities. The argument for efficiency-improving corruption is a simple extension of this idea (Bardhan, 1997, p. 1322).

It is possible to object to this line of thought by emphasizing, again, that the Efficiency Frontier and, *pari passu*, the efficiency standard, are indeterminate. And it is possible, were this objection to be set aside, to argue that efficiency is a peculiar standard by which to judge unethical behavior. Moreover, it is possible, as was suggested above, to object that the implicit endorsement of corruption is irreconcilable with *any* understanding of justice, whether rights-protection, mutual advantage, or impartiality. Ultimately, however, more is at issue. As the philosopher Roger Scruton has suggested,

> . . . through the theory of consequentialism, the possibility of unlimited corruption has re-entered the modern conscience and produced some interesting casuistry in 'applied ethics' (1994, p. 283).

Granting this, perhaps the essential point is that, because SWT is consequence-based and procedurally-detached, the propensity to 'justify' *any* means to achieve 'efficient' outcomes should come as no surprise. Indeed, the fact that utilitarian SWT cannot regard rights as having moral force militates against any understanding of rights as side-constraints on action. As we saw in section 5.3, 'only consequences for individual well-being matter, with other items such as rights or virtues viewed strictly as means to promoting welfare' (Hausman and McPherson, 1993, p. 704). That such an approach is questionable on ethical grounds is self-evident. That it may be employed to guide public policy formulation is, at best, problematic.

8.4 Efficiency and the 'Transition'

If it is possible to argue that the unintended consequences of the application of SWT subsume the endorsement of government corruption and an expansion of government beyond that which 'could be justified on scientific grounds', the same might not be said of what has been styled the 'standard reform prescription for an ex-socialist country' (Murrell, 1995, p. 164). While proponents of SWT might argue that the 'progovernment and prointerference' and 'corruption' problems are aberrational,[7] they clearly cannot sustain this argument when attention shifts to the 'transition' of ex-socialist countries. Indeed, a 'striking degree of unanimity' has emerged with respect to this issue:

> . . . the standard reform prescription . . . is to proceed as fast as possible on macroeconomic stabilization, the liberalization of domestic trade and prices, current account convertibility, privatization, and the creation of a social safety net, while simultaneously creating the legal framework for a market economy (Murrell, 1995, p. 164).

Implicit in this portmanteau of policy prescriptions is the notion that 'efficiency' is the appropriate evaluative standard.[8] Indeed, while Professor Murrell is critical of the received approach, he emphasizes that

> Questions of how property rights are established, secured, and efficiently reassigned are often downplayed when examining stable capitalist societies, or they receive mundane technical answers. These questions generate new interest and new forms when examining a society that has only informal, unclear, and tangled property rights. There is a need to understand which formalization of stakeholder rights affords the highest probability of efficient bargains being struck in the future. Clarification of the role of customary property rights in economic activity is essential. One must grasp exactly why politically inspired interventions (or corruption) reduce economic efficiency. Reformers must ask which process is likely to lead to the formation of a social consensus that endorses a system of secure property rights (1995, pp. 170-171).

While much can be said about this, it is clear that the instrumental role of efficiency is a recurring theme. Interestingly, the passage also invokes the notion that corruption and 'politically inspired interventions' reduce economic efficiency. Suffice it to say that this perception is difficult to reconcile with the view, already noted, that 'in the context of pervasive and cumbersome regulations in developing countries, corruption may actually improve efficiency and help growth'.

Putting this issue aside, the essential point is that, because the received SWT is both institutionless and intendedly value-free, it is not surprising that the standard 'transition' prescription

> . . . begins at the end point, an idealized market, phrasing everything in those terms, ignoring the crucial question of how reforms engage existing society. The project of the economist is to grasp the tabula rasa and design a new system, to match events against the yardstick of that design, and to diagnose as failures any deviations from design (Murrell, 1995, p. 177).

In effect, the efficiency-driven transition contemplates an institutional tabula rasa; a society for which the major institutional imperative is the creation of a 'legal framework for a market economy'.

As the discussion in earlier chapters suggests, this is a circumspect view of the world. *Inter alia*, the standard reform approach neglects the intervention of informal rules of the game:

> In transition economics, rulers implemented far-reaching transformation of formal rules of the game to institute market economies. Economic analyses of transition economies tend to focus on the changes in the institutional framework resulting in (and from) the dismantling of state control over economic activity. . . .
>
> But . . . the behavior of economic actors frequently bears little resemblance to the legitimate courses of action stipulated by the formal rules. Instead, networks based on personal connections serve to organize market-oriented economic behavior according to informal norms reflecting the private expectations of entrepreneurs and politicians. They act in the shadow of the state. . . . (Nee, 1998, pp. 85-86).

It would seem, in short, that a society 'in transition' is not an institutional tabula rasa. Both formal and informal rules of the game affect, and are affected by, the transition process. Moreover, the formal and informal institutions extant at a cross-section of time are path-dependent; they reflect, *inter alia*, an intertemporal learning process (North, 1994, pp. 359-360). Granting this, it appears that to apply the efficiency standard without taking explicit account of extant and evolving institutions is to commit a serious error of omission. The error may, in fact, account for the lack of useful advice to which Professor Demsetz refers:

> As has been made apparent from the lack of useful advice from Western econo-
> mists to policy makers in Eastern Europe attempting to convert economies from
> communism to capitalism, we know much less about our institutions, or, at least,
> much less about creating them, than our predecessors presumed (1997, p. 11).

If, as Demsetz suggests, economists know little about institutions, it may be partly attributable to their predilection to conduct 'value-free' analysis. *Inter alia*, 'scientific' or positive economic analysis is not congenial to the notion that 'culture' and the 'economy' exert reciprocal influences. Yet it seems clear that

> Culture is not a given, economics is not necessarily divorced from the cultural
> context, but nor is culture exempt from economic influence. . . . (Jones, 1995, pp.
> 277-278).

The basic relevance of culture to economic behavior and, *pari passu*, to the 'transition' becomes clear once the nature of culture is understood

> The term 'culture' is osmotic, covering all the usual artifacts and personal and
> social behaviors, but also alluding to values (such as trust, honesty or complex
> systems of religious values) and models of organization of the kinds that are
> starting to attract attention as disembodied 'institutions' (Jones, 1995, p. 271).

The point, in short, is not simply that culture is path-dependent, or that culture both affects, and is affected by, economic interaction. From the point of view of the transition process, account must be taken of the fact that culture sub-sumes such values as trust and honesty; values which, in turn, are essential lubricants of a market economy. Given this understanding, appeals to the notion of 'efficiency-enhancing corruption' are clearly inappropriate. Quite the opposite. To paraphrase Professor Buchanan, there may be circumstances -- such as those of an economy 'in transition'--in which the requisite cultural values may have to be 'cultivated'.[9] The failure to acknowledge this funda-mental fact is not simply a theoretical lacuna. It is a serious debility, especially when SWT is invoked to guide the transition from a socialist to a market economy. As Professor North has emphasized,

There is nothing automatic about the evolving of conditions that will permit low-cost transacting in the impersonal market that are essential to productive economies. . . . Creating the institutions that will alter the benefit/cost ratios in favor of cooperation in impersonal exchange is a complex process, because it not only entails the creation of economic institutions, but requires that they be undergirded by appropriate political institutions (1994, p. 365).

The essential point is that the transition to a market economy contemplates *both* the institutionalization and the protection of instrumentally important and morally exigent rights. That this is so follows, *inter alia*, from the fact that the passage toward a market economy involves increasingly impersonal transactions (Alchian et al, 1996, p. 417). While it is possible under such conditions partially to rely on contractually-derived formal rules, the instrumental role of ethical norms cannot be denied. Endogenously generated ethical constraints do not simply discourage opportunistic behavior and, *pari passu*, reduce transaction costs. They also engender trust; a value which, as I have suggested, is both essential to the functioning of a market economy, and antithetical to the notion of 'efficiency-enhancing corruption'. Granting this, account must be taken of the interrelationships among morality, confidence, trust, and the institutional framework of market economies:

> [An] interesting aspect of transaction costs is that their level depends, *inter alia*, on the behavior of individuals. Monitoring and enforcement costs, in particular, will tend to be low if mutual trust predominates in the society. Under favorable conditions, property rights will be respected, and comparatively uniform ideas will exist about the nature of fair solutions to conflicts. It would seem, then, that social morality, confidence, trust, and the institutional framework are all inter-related. The expenses of public education, and of motivating people, have to be viewed, in part, as contributions that bring about lesser 'frictions' (transaction costs) in society and enhance economic productivity (Furubotn and Richter, 1997, p. 49).

What has been suggested reduces to this: SWT is an inappropriate guide to transition policy. The indeterminancy of its key theoretical constructs is a threshold problem. Yet, even when these problems are set aside, 'efficiency' is, occasionally, invoked to rationalize behavior which is inconsistent with values which are understood to be instrumental to the functioning of market economies. Moreover, given its institutional paucity, the efficiency-driven transition is excessively reliant on the notion that a legal framework is a necessary condition for what Prybyla has called 'modernization' (1995). While it is a necessary condition, it is not a sufficient condition. Informal 'rules of the game' must also be operative. And these rules--including ethical constraints--may have to be cultivated. Given that 'the past rules the present, that history matters' (Furubotn and Richter, 1997, p. 26), the inculcation of ethical norms may require that "Social morality (or trust) . . . be produced through 'education'--a collective undertaking that requires a considerable amount of real resources and time. . . ." (Furubotn and Richter, 1997, p. 21). As we have seen, while this appreciation is central to Buchanan's contractarian or constitutional political economy approach, it is not reconcilable with institutionless, intendedly value-free SWT.

Finally, the fact that some social welfare theorists argue that observed, unethical behavior may be efficiency-enhancing indirectly underscores still another brute fact: In a world of 'frictions'--of bounded rationality and information asymmetries--opportunistic behavior will always be observable, no matter which formal and informal constraints are operative. Granting this, attention should center on crafting transparent institutional structures. At issue is not simply 'uninhibited access by all transactors to information . . . the elimination of secrecy and opacity from the economic structure' (Prybyla, 1995, p. 5). At issue is the rudimentary fact that

> . . . the effectiveness of markets (in which people are free to pursue individual self-interest) depends on a political system that successfully constrains individuals from pursuing self-interest through political channels. . . .
>
> The very origins of successful markets are seen to be dependent on institutional constraints on political actors (Miller, 1997, p. 1198).[10]

The need for transparency and for institutional constraints on political actors suggests that, while democracy 'works best for economic growth' (Prybyla, 1995, p. 19), the institutions of democratic government must be carefully constructed. Central to this understanding is the notion that rights and their correlative duties must be respected. Yet, if rights are given lexical priority, both constitutional and policy decisions must regard justice--in the sense of impartiality--as both instrumentally important and morally exigent.[11] 'Trust', after all, is partly dependent upon the perception that transactions, solutions to conflicts, and government policies are 'fair'. The essential point is that 'Concentration on the morality of ends, can and has been used to justify unworthy ends' (Prybyla, 1993, p. 7). For these and other reasons discussed in earlier chapters, consequence-based, procedurally-detached analysis is ill-suited to the constitutional political economy project. What is required is a procedural approach which both respects rights and justice and, subject to endogenously determined ethical constraints, enables agents to pursue their own ends--whatever they may be. In short, what is required is democracy with procedural checks, balances and guarantees:

> It is precisely the genius of the American Constitution that its procedural checks, balances, and guarantees stem from a clear recognition of the fundamental importance of the morality of means (Prybyla, 1993, p. 7).[12]

It is for these and other reasons elaborated above that (contractarian) constitutional political economy concentrates on the morality of means.

8.5 Contractarian Analysis: A Constraint on Leviathan

It is appropriate, first, to anticipate an objection to contractarian analysis of political institutions. While it is true that the analysis is procedural, it is not consequence-detached. The essential idea is that (contractarian) constitutional political economy seeks an institutional structure which assigns lexical priority to rights and, at the same time, regards justice as impartiality. Both of these are, to paraphrase Hausman and McPherson, well-defined consequentialist goals (1993, p. 707). Moreover, the approach emphasizes that individuals shall be free--subject to endogenously determined ethical constraints--to pursue their goals, 'whatever they may be'.[13] That these goals cannot be known *a priori* follows from the fact that agents' multiple preference and value structures are both unidentified and mutable. In effect, the constitutional political economy approach envisions a decision environment in which, *inter alia*, choice, self-determination, agency and independence are respected. These, too, may be broadly understood to be consequentialist goals. That said, the emphasis here is upon procedural constraints on government action. The ideas which animate this procedural concern are by now familiar. *Inter alia*, the 'frictions' which characterize objective reality are congenial to the emergence of opportunistic behavior on the part both of principal-voters and their elected and bureaucratic agents. At the most rudimentary level, prospective beneficiaries of government spending programs appreciate that, whereas the benefits will be concentrated, the costs of such programs will be widely dispersed. This concentrated benefit-dispersed cost phenomenon was described at the end of the nineteenth century by Vilfredo Pareto:

> Let us suppose that in a country of thirty million inhabitants it is proposed . . . to get each citizen to pay out one franc a year, and to distribute the total amount

amongst thirty persons. . . . The two groups will differ greatly in their response to this situation. Those who hope to gain. . . . will win newspapers over to their interest by financial inducements and drum up support from all quarters. A discreet hand will warm the palms of needy legislators, even of ministers. . . .

On the other hand, the despoiled are much less active. . . . for such people, there is the likelihood that their political contribution to the campaign against the spoilation will exceed the total amount they stand to lose by the measure in question. . . .

Those who hope to gain. . . . have agents everywhere, who descend in swarms on the electorate, urging the voters that sound and enlightened patriotism calls for the success of their modest proposal. . . .

In these circumstances the outcome is not in doubt; the spoilators will win hands down (1896).[14]

The point is not that all participants in conflictual or ordinary politics should be presumed to be 'knaves'. Rather, the presumption must be that potential beneficiaries of government spending (or tax or other) programs have incentive to exploit a situation in which information asymmetries are pervasive, decision and monitoring costs are high, and those who bear the costs either are unaware, or have incentive to 'free-ride'; to allow others to bear the monitoring costs. Granting all of this, it appears that governmental budget processes are subject to a spending bias which is difficult to contain, given bounded rationality and all that it implies.

At issue here is not the 'optimal size' of government. From the perspective of constitutional political economy this cannot be determined *a priori*. Rather, the 'size' and composition of government activity are determined by conflictual or ordinary politics, subject both to constraints imposed at the constitutional stage, and to endogenously determined ethical constraints, some of which may have to be cultivated. While, as was suggested in Chapter 7, this indeterminancy may be troublesome to some, constitutional political economy does not seek to 'explain' the origins of rules or the emergence of particular policy initiatives. Rather, because it offers a basis for normative appraisal, the analysis is justificatory. Whereas SWT focuses on 'efficient' outcomes, constitutional political economy assesses competing institutional arrangements and policy decisions along two moral dimensions: Rules and policies must both respect rights and their correlative duties, and be 'fair' in the sense of impartiality.

Putting the issue of rights attenuation aside, at least for the moment, it seems clear that the spending bias to which Pareto and others refer reflects, *inter alia*, impulses which are not congruent with impartiality. By definition, Pareto's 'spoilators' seek advantages, the costs of which are to be borne by the 'despoiled'. While the 'selfish' impulse cannot be 'legislated away', constitutional political economy suggests that attention might appropriately center on a constitutional remedy. Simply stated, consideration might be given to embedding a spending restraint in the Constitution; the document which establishes the rules of the game within which conflictual politics is engaged. Moreover, because transparency is important both to the realization and the perception of fairness, deliberations at the constitutional stage should also contemplate a prohibition against omnibus spending bills. The core idea is that a requirement to vote seriatim on individual spending bills would serve to pierce the cloak of secrecy 'behind which special interests can most effectively advance their interests, outside of public scrutiny' (Stiglitz, 1998, p. 16). While these constitutionally imposed restraints could not directly reduce the monitoring costs to which I earlier referred, the time expended in consideration of individual spending bills would serve an additional purpose: Given a binding time constraint, fewer spending bills could be considered. This elementary fact would serve, indirectly, to reduce the attendant monitoring costs.[15] Granting this, the confluence of heightened transparency and reduced monitoring costs could be expected to alter the incentive structure in favor of just--in the sense of impartial--outcomes.[16]

The probability of the emergence of just outcomes may be enhanced in other ways. The developing literature on campaign contributions is heuristic. Professor Robert Florence has summarized the situation in this way:

Increased participation by pressure groups in the political process over the last two decades has become obvious even to the casual observer. . . .

. . . it is not surprising [therefore] that the scholarly analysis of campaign contributions has seen its most significant increases in the last decade. . . . It is also not surprising that the popular press and the public seem convinced that special interest groups (via [political action committees]) are buying votes in Congress to further their agendas (1999, p. 59).

That this *perception* is corrosive of trust and, *mutatis mutandis*, of the perceived legitimacy of the political process, is self-evident. But what is ultimately at issue is the *empirical* relationship--if any--between political action committee (PAC) contributions and legislative effort on behalf of PACs.

With this in mind, it is useful first to determine which legislator attributes account for differences in PAC contributions. Professor Florence's empirical results--employing campaign contributions from PACs representing the aerospace, airline, automobile, and oil industries--suggest that

> . . . there is evidence that is consistent with the conventional theory of the importance of committee membership. Moreover, the evidence is stronger still that leadership on committees (in the Senate) is a powerful driver of campaign contributions. The results for party affiliation are mixed (Florence, 1999, p. 71).

That the evidence supports the 'conventional theory of the importance of committee membership' is perhaps not surprising. It is well known that legislation affecting a particular industry emanates from the committee(s) with legislative and oversight jurisdiction. That committee leadership should be 'a powerful driver' of PAC contributions also comports with intuition. Simply stated, the committee chairman determines--*sometimes* in consultation with the committee's ranking minority member--the committee's agenda. If these empirical results are, therefore, not surprising, the question remains: Is there a relationship between PAC contributions and legislative effort on behalf of the contributing PACs? Empirical results relating to financial-services legislation motivated Kroszner and Stratmann to develop the following theory of congressional organization:

> According to our theory, legislators desire the formation of specialized standing committees, with the ability to stay on committees as long as they wish, in order to alleviate agency problems due to the inability to write direct fee-for-service contracts. Committees foster repeated interactions, reputation building, and long-term relationships between the interest groups and members of the relevant committee, thereby increasing the likelihood that a high-contribution, high-legislative effort equilibrium will exist (1998, pp. 1182-1183).

While scholars may question the empirical results and, or, the *ex post* rationalization of the findings, this much can be said: What is at issue is not simply the growth of government. The issue of ultimate concern is the impartiality of spending (and other) decisions. Considered in this light, the *possibility* that the congressional committee structure facilitates the emergence of a 'high-contribution, high-legislative effort equilibrium' should be cause for concern. Granting this, and given that 'the public seem(s) convinced that special interest groups . . . are buying votes in Congress' (Florence, 1999, p. 59), the solution-- if one is needed--does not lie in conflictual or ordinary politics. Plainly stated, rules and procedural changes emanating from a legislative body may be transitory:

> The problem of commitment stems from the inherent nature of government itself. Government is the primary enforcer of contracts. It uses its monopoly power on the legal use of force to create the possibility of private commitment. There is no one, however, whose job it is to guard the guardian. The government cannot make commitments because it always has the possibility of changing its mind, and earlier 'agreements' cannot be enforced (Stiglitz, 1998, pp. 9-10).

Thus, while in early 1995 the United States House of Representatives adopted changes in rules and procedures which contemplated, *inter alia*, term limits on the tenure of committee and subcommittee chairmen (Staff, January 6, 1995), these procedural changes were subject to change *during* the 104th and subsequent Congresses.[17] To the extent that the public is convinced that 'special interest groups . . . are buying votes in Congress', and that, *pari passu*, spending outcomes are not impartial, the appropriate remedy is constitutional. While predicting the precise outlines of such a remedy lies outside the scope of constitutional political economy, attention might appropriately center on the number of permissible committees, on the tenure of committee chairmen, members, and committee staff, and on the 'revolving door' phenomenon (whereby committee members and staff secure employment with entities whose activities are contemplated by the committee's jurisdiction).[18]

If the focus of constitutional or inclusive politics might appropriately center on congressional committee organization, the same might be said of executive branch departments, agencies and bureaus. The following example is illustrative of the issues involved.

In its February 1988 *Economic Report of the President*, the President's Council of Economic Advisers observed that

> [Between 1981 and 1986] the number of petitions resulting in interventions . . . increased 258 percent [relative to the 1975-1980 period]. It is difficult to believe . . . that dumping has risen to more than two and one-half times its previous level (especially since the strong dollar during the latter period made selling to the United States easier for foreigners rather than harder). More likely, the higher intervention rate derives from changes in U.S. trade law in 1979, the large trade deficit, and the consequent increased demand for protection inside this country (1988, p. 159).

At issue here are anti-dumping interventions by the United States government. 'Dumping' is defined in international trade law as selling in a national market below production cost or below export-country domestic prices. Under United States law the Department of Commerce's International Trade Administration [ITA] determines whether dumping has occurred. The International Trade Commission [ITC] then determines whether a U.S. industry has been 'materially injured' by the dumped imports. If, in their 'final determinations' both ITA and ITC rule affirmatively, duties equal to the 'dumping margins' are placed on the 'unfairly-priced' imports.

With this background it is clear that, in February 1988, the Council of Economic Advisers was concerned about the effect of the 'increased demand for protection inside this country' on the ITA-ITC anti-dumping investigative process. And there was and still is cause for concern.

Whereas, in principle, the ITC commissioners are insulated from political pressure,[19] there is an important sense in which they are not 'independent'. The ITC is responsible to two congressional oversight committees. Both the Senate Finance Committee and the House Ways and Means Trade Subcommittee have jurisdiction over legislation affecting the ITC. And, equally important, the Congress controls the ITC's budget.

Not surprisingly, there is evidence that the Congress generally, and the two oversight committees particularly, influence ITC decisions. A recent study concluded that

> ... the evidence ... suggests that the ITC has been an imperfect barrier between vote-seeking politicians and protection-seeking interests. ... The success of an industry in obtaining relief in the anti-dumping process depends on the objective facts of the petition, whether the industry has low-wage workers and, finally, on the influence of their elected representatives. Those fortunate enough to be represented by 'strategically' placed politicians, i.e., Congressmen with direct influence over the administrating bureaucracy, are more likely to be successful in obtaining protection (Moore, 1992, p. 465).

While it might be argued that, in a representative democracy, Members of Congress 'with direct influence over the administrating bureaucracy' *ought* to influence the anti-dumping petition process, it might also be argued that the process should be immunized from *political* pressure. *In principle*, both the ITA's and the ITC's determinations can be developed based upon the objective facts of each case. It is in any case clear that, if the public is, indeed, 'convinced that special interests ... are buying votes in Congress to further their agendas', a politicized anti-dumping process further erodes trust in government. The central issue is, to paraphrase Stiglitz, Whose job is it to guard the guardian? If the members of congressional oversight committees are excessively responsive to special interests' protectionist or other demands, who is it that provides the requisite oversight? It seems clear that a statutory remedy would be unavailing, both because of the commitment problem, and because of information asymmetry. Given that anti-dumping petitioners, the ITA, the ITC and the oversight committees possess information which the general public does not possess, it is difficult for voter-principals to determine whether a finding reflects the 'facts' or the 'politics' of the case. Indeed, it is possible to argue that

> ... since 'expert' arguments [cannot] be well evaluated by the electorate. ... we have established independent agencies in many areas to move critical parts of decision-making at least slightly further from the political scene (Stiglitz, 1998, p. 17).

In effect, this is an acknowledgment that voter-principals *cannot* provide the requisite oversight. Granting this, a fundamental issue must be addressed: In a world of increasing complexity, bounded rationality, information asymmetries, and opportunistic behavior, how far should anti-dumping and other government decisions be removed from political influence? As Stiglitz suggests, this is an 'arena in which democratic processes and rational decision-making seemingly come into conflict, [and] in which the resolution is not so apparent' (1998, p. 17). Yet, if the solution is not apparent, it does seem clear that objective features of observable reality militate against a statutory solution. What seems to be required is a constitutional remedy; a remedy which can only emerge if voter-principals engage in inclusive, rather than conflictual politics, and set out explicitly to codify the constitutional rules of the game within which anti-dumping and other government decision-making unfolds.

The discussion to this point has been animated by concern that government spending and other decisions be just and, therefore, impartial. If a case can be made that government spending decisions are not impartial, the same may be said of government tax policy. The essential problem is that the sheer complexity of the tax code--and of the budget process generally--contributes to, and is a reflection of, opportunistic behavior on the part of special interests (Pareto's 'spoilators') and legislators:

> The budgets of modern economies, particularly those of countries with large public sectors, are very complex. Politicians do not have an incentive to adopt the most transparent practices. Lack of transparency helps to create confusion and ambiguity on the real state of public finances, by hiding as much as possible of the current and future tax burdens, overemphasizing the benefits of spending, and

underestimating the extent of current and future government liabilities (Alesina and Perotti, 1996, p. 403).

The 'lack of transparency' is manifested in arcane budget process law[20] and in 'the manner in which so much decision-making occurs--the secrecy, the midnight committee meetings. . . .'--all of which contribute 'both to the perception and reality of asymmetrical information' (Stiglitz, 1998, p. 15). And it is precisely this environment of (partially) contrived information asymmetry which is both corrosive of trust and congenial to preferential treatment:

> In a world of secrecy, you will always suspect that some interest group is taking advantage of the secrecy to advance their cause over yours, to steal, if not directly from you personally, more broadly from the public. Why else the secrecy? There is plenty of evidence to support these anxieties; the special tax provisions put into every tax bill at the last moment are perhaps the most glaring example (Stiglitz, 1998, p. 15).

By one estimate--proffered by the Majority Leader of the United States House of Representatives--some 67,000 lobbyists work to ensure that often obscure tax code changes benefit their clients (Armey, June 19, 1996). Whether this estimate is accurate is not the central issue. What is clear is that neither the procedures nor the outcomes which characterize the tax policy process can reasonably be characterized as impartial. Indeed, if a tax code consisting, in part, of surreptitiously codified preferential provisions does not comport with an intuitive sense of impartiality, it is quite removed from John Rawls' understanding of an impartial 'tax scheme':

> . . . since the burden of taxation is to be justly shared and it aims at establishing just arrangements. . . . a proportional expenditure tax may be part of the best tax scheme. . . . (1971, p. 278).

While, as Rawls himself suggests, this leaves many complications aside, the core idea is that impartiality is antithetical to preferential treatment. Yet, given the commitment problem and the information asymmetry inherent in conflictual politics, it is unlikely that an impartial 'tax scheme' is likely, permanently, to emerge from any statutory process. If voter-principals are, indeed, concerned that 'some interest group is taking advantage of the secrecy to advance their cause' over others, then *something like* a proportional expenditure tax should have to be embedded in the Constitution.

The same might be said of distribution policies. Given the lexical priority of rights, distribution policies should be impartial. Whether this contemplates an equal distribution of primary social goods (as Rawls suggests), or of opportunities (as Buchanan suggests), the characteristics of the conflictual political process suggest that the chosen distribution rules should be embedded in the Constitution. While, as always, the precise nature of the rules which emerge from the inclusive or constitutional political process is indeterminate, this much can be said: The institutionalization and maintenance of distributive rules which seek intertemporally to equalize the distribution of primary social goods or of opportunities will, eventually, reduce the need for distribution policies. Given a Kantian commitment to the moral equivalence of persons, this is morally exigent. And, if Temple is right, that high inequality is both harmful for economic growth and for social and political stability (1999, pp. 146 and 152), it may also be instrumentally important.

If a Kantian commitment to the treatment of persons as 'ends in themselves' demands that we promote impartial institutions, it also demands that we respect persons' freedom to act. *Given* this prior commitment, Rawls and Buchanan assign lexical priority to rights. On this account--a view shared by constitutional political economists--rights are both morally exigent and instrumentally important. It follows that rights and their correlative duties must be respected.

Let us first stipulate that the analysis of rights is complicated. While the Kantian perspective answers one question--How can rights be justified?--other questions must be answered. *Inter alia*, we should like to know: (1) What or who can be the subject of a right?; (2) What kind of things can there be a right to?; (3) Are rights inalienable?; (4) Are rights ever absolute? (Almond, 1993, pp. 261-262). Moreover, as we have seen, rights may be regarded, at one extreme, as absolute side constraints on action or as 'trumps', and, at the other extreme, as merely instrumental. And, finally, following Hohfeld (1919), it is recognized that rights involve complex clusters of permissions and constraints regarding the actions of individuals. On this account, rights may contemplate claims, powers, liberties, and immunities (Almond, 1993, p. 262).[21]

Granting all of this, the view that rights are not seen as the basis of protection for *all* human interests, but rather 'for those specifically related to choice, self-determination, agency and independence' captures only a part of the individual's moral personality. While, as we have seen, this view is related to laissez-faire and minimalist theories of the state, the analysis of rights and correlative duties contemplates a broader understanding of moral personality.

Given this broader context, how are we to understand the lexical priority of rights? On Rawls' account,

. . . liberty can only be restricted for the sake of liberty. There are two cases:

(a) a less extensive liberty must strengthen the total system of liberty shared by all;

(b) a less than equal liberty must be acceptable to those with the lesser liberty (1971, p. 302).

From the perspective of constitutional political economy, the analysis of rights must, then, be predicated upon the following basic understanding: *Given the moral equivalence of persons, rights must be given lexical priority in the sense that, whereas rights may, in principle, be attenuated, rights restrictions must be justified.*[22] Either the restriction(s) must strengthen the 'total system of liberty shared by all', or 'a less than equal liberty must be acceptable' to those whose rights are attenuated.

Recognizing the inherent complexity of rights analysis, and given the Kantian/Rawlsian understanding of the lexical priority of rights, what does anecdotal and empirical evidence drawn from United States' experience tell us? It is appropriate, first, to acknowledge that much of what may be styled the 'erosion of rights' literature may most appropriately be characterized as heuristic. Employing a commonly invoked proxy for the 'growth of government' and, on his view, the concomitant erosion of freedom, James Bovard has observed that

Federal agencies publish an average of over 200 pages of new rulings, regulations, and proposals in the *Federal Register* each business day. The growth of the federal statute book is one of the clearest measures of the increase of the government control of the citizenry (1995, p. 1).

While fundamental questions attach to this characterization of events, it seems clear that the proliferation of rules and regulations contemplates the attenuation of affected parties' exchange, property, contract or other rights. Given the lexical priority of rights, it is appropriate to ask, How are these interventions justified? Granting the logic of what has been said in earlier chapters, an 'efficiency' argument of the sort contemplated by a regulatory budget is unavailing:

The [Joint Economic] Committee urges Congress and the Executive Branch to study and develop a regulatory budget during the next 3 years, with emphasis on developing the methodology necessary to make a regulatory budget for the Federal Government a reality in the future. A regulatory budget would encourage government agencies to reduce the costs of regulation and improve the efficiency of regulatory programs. In addition, a regulatory budget would supplement the annual fiscal budget to give the public, Congress, and the President a more comprehensive view of the Federal Government's command over resources for public purposes (Bentsen, 1980, p. 47).

Promulgated as 'Recommendation No. 12' in the Joint Economic Committee's unanimous 1980 annual *Report* to Congress, the proposed regulatory budget emphasizes the need to 'improve the efficiency of regulatory programs'.[23] Whatever else is said, given the indeterminancy of the efficiency standard, neither a regulatory budget nor the invocation of 'benefit-cost' calculations can 'justify' a regulatory initiative.[24] In any case, insofar as a 'regulation' contemplates the attenuation of exchange, property, contract or other rights, the justification must either be that the regulation strengthens the 'total system of liberty shared by all', *or* that the implied less than equal liberty is 'acceptable to those with the [resultant] lesser liberty'.

It is safe to say that neither the body of regulatory law nor the Executive Orders which have charged the Executive Branch with assessing the 'benefits and costs' of regulation contemplate the lexical priority of rights. Moreover, given the commitment and transparency problems associated with conflictual politics, it is not clear that statutes embodying a liberty-based justificatory requirement would have more than a transitory effect. Granting this, it seems appropriate that such a requirement be embedded in the Constitution. While such a constitutionally-mandated requirement would, inevitably force the Congress, the Executive Branch, and, ultimately, the courts, to grapple with difficult rights-related issues, there is a sense in which this is precisely what is required. Continued reliance on an efficiency justification of regulatory initiatives is inappropriate, given the indeterminancy of the efficiency standard, and given that its application has sometimes led economists into the trap of assuming that, 'if the market fails, the government is sure to do better'.[25]

Chapter 7 concluded with Professor Buchanan's admonition that

Normatively, the task of the constitutional political economist is to assist individuals, as citizens who ultimately control their own social order, in their continuing search for those rules of the political game that will best serve their purposes, whatever they may be (1987, p. 250).

The argument for constitutional revision developed above has been proffered in this spirit. While many objections may be raised, perhaps the most profound has been suggested by Sandmo (1990, p. 63): 'In current policy debates we are clearly not in a situation that resembles the constitutional stage'. To this objection, I offer the following rejoinder: Given that the efficiency standard is indeterminate, often misused, irreconcilable with the moral force of rights, and unable to accommodate any plausible understanding of justice, 'something else' is required. Then, *if* one regards persons as moral equals possessed of unidentified and mutable preference and value structures, consequence-based, procedurally-detached analysis is unavailing. Given that each person should be free to pursue his goals--whatever they may be[26]--attention must center on institutional arrangements which are both impartial and respectful of the lexical priority of rights. That this project must involve inclusive or constitutional, rather than conflictual politics is a corollary of the 'frictions' which characterize the 'real world' decision environment. To paraphrase Pareto, opportunistic spoilators will always seek to benefit at the expense of the despoiled.

Notes

1   Indeed, in view of the prisoner's dilemma problem, and given that utilitarian arguments can always be deployed to overcome any 'commitment', it is not clear that SWT can accommodate the view of justice as mutual advantage.

2   As we have seen, Professor Sen's revision of the received SWT contemplates both consequences and procedures. That said, there are problems with his suggested approach. See section 7.3, above.

3   See section, 5.2, above.

4   See section 4.5, above, for a discussion of the fundamental theorems of welfare economics.

5   See Chapters 4 and 5, above.

6   Narrow self-interest and the constrained maximization postulate have been invoked by other economists to rationalize corrupt behavior on the part of politicians and government officials. Cheung has asserted, for example, that

> . . . all individuals, government officials and politicians without exception, are constrained self-maximizers . . . . each and every politician and government official has only one priority in mind. Just like you and me, they get up in the morning and think about how to produce more income for themselves, and under the usual social and political constraints corruption is generally the most convenient avenue to achieve the goal (1996, p. 1).

Continuing, Cheung insists that

> Any other way of thinking is inconsistent with the postulate of constrained maximization. In other words, any other argument shows no faith in mankind (1996, p. 3).

7   I would argue that these phenomena are not aberrations.

8   Arguably, appeal to the need for creation of a 'social safety net' is motivated by concern that the efficiency-driven transformation process will create 'losers' as well as 'winners' and that, absent such a safety net, the 'losers' may resist, and ultimately derail, the transformation process.

9   See, for example, Buchanan , 1994b, p. 62.
10   See also Furubotn and Richter, 1997, pp. 417-420 and Prybyla, 1993. In contrast, for some
      economists for whom 'the market' is both preeminent and the desired outcome of a 'reform
      process', 'politics that widen market space have something to recommend them, even when
      repression is used to produce that outcome' (Barber, 1995, p. 1947). Once again, the
      consequentialist view that only outcomes matter, and that desired outcomes are to be
      promoted without taking account of the means by which the outcomes are secured is the
      core problem. Paradoxically, the acceptance of 'governmental nastiness' in pursuit of 'the
      market' is sometimes ascribed to the 'Chicago Boys', the Chilean economists trained in
      what has been styled 'hardcore neoclassicism'; a paradigm which, as we have emphasized,
      is grounded in choice, self-determination, agency, independence, and the notion of a
      minimalist government. See Barber, 1995, p. 1947.
11   Indeed, on one account, 'The legitimacy of government is determined (we normally think)
      by the justice of its actions . . . .' (Kymlicka, 1993, p. 187).
12   See also Buchanan, 1987, p. 250.
13   Emphasis is placed on the intervention of endogenously determined ethical constraints,
      inter alia, because I share Professor Sen's view that 'the possibility of having unacceptable
      consequences has to be addressed by any . . . procedural system' (1995, p. 12). See also
      Sandmo, 1990, p. 58.
14   Pareto's view comports with Professor Buchanan's contemporary assessment

      . . . there seems to arise a natural proclivity for individuals, groups, and the political
      entrepreneurs who represent them, to extend the range and scope of collective-political
      action beyond any conceivable publicness boundaries . . . . The arms, agencies and
      authority of the state will be utilized to secure, or in attempts to secure, differential
      gains for members of political coalitions, with little or no regard for normatively
      appropriate boundaries on governmental action (1986, pp. 254-255).

      For a dissenting view, that 'democratic processes elicit . . . (less self-interested) behavior',
      see Cullis and Jones, 1998.
15   Whether a constitutionally-mandated spending restraint should also contemplate a
      'balanced budget' requirement is a separate issue. See, for example, Buchanan and
      Wagner, 1977.
16   As has been repeatedly emphasized, 'preaching' may have a role to play in the endogenous
      generation of ethical constraints on opportunistic behavior.
17   The same 'commitment' problem applies to statutory procedural changes: 'Statutory con-
      straints remain effective only so long as no majority coalition forms to repeal the statutory
      constraints' (Hatch, 1981, p. 42).
18   The tenure of staff is also an important consideration, given that *their* 'repeated
      interactions, reputation building and long-term relationships' with interest groups may
      facilitate the emergence of a 'high-contribution, high-legislative effort equilibrium'.
19   The six commissioners are appointed by the President, confirmed by the Senate, and serve
      non-renewable, nine-year terms.
20   For a discussion of the complexity of the budget process and of the implications for voter
      oversight, see Roth, 1994, esp. Chapter 1.
21   See also Hausman and McPherson, 1996, pp. 125-126.
22   The implicit idea is that rights may be linked to liberty or 'freedom'. This seems plausible,
      inter alia, because rights determine the distribution of freedom (Hausman and McPherson,
      1993, p. 695).

23   The regulatory budget idea has appeared in several forms, most recently in the House Republicans' September 27, 1994 'Contract With America'.
24   For a discussion of 'Regulation: Costs and Benefits', see Office of Management and Budget, 1999, pp. 279-281.
25   See section 8.2, above.
26   Subject, as always, to endogenously determined ethical constraints.

Bibliography

Aaron, H.J. (1994), 'Public Policy, Values, and Consciousness', *Journal of Economic Perspectives*, vol. 8, pp. 3-21.

Alchian, A.A., Buchanan, J.M., Demsetz, H., Leijonhufvud, A., Lott, J.R., Jr., Sharpe, W.F., and Topel, R.H. (1996), 'In Celebration of Armen Alchian's 80th Birthday: Living and Breathing Economics', *Economic Inquiry*, vol. 34, pp. 412-426.

Alesina, A. and Perotti, R. (1996), 'Fiscal Discipline and the Budget Process', *American Economic Association Papers and Proceedings*, vol. 86, pp. 401-407.

Almond, B. (1993), 'Rights', in P. Singer (ed), *A Companion to Ethics*, Blackwell Publishers, Ltd, Cambridge, MA, pp. 259-269.

Armey, D. (Rep.) (June 19, 1996), 'How Taxes Corrupt', *The Wall Street Journal*.

Arrow, K.J. (1951), *Social Choice and Individual Values*, Yale University Press, New Haven.

Barber, W.J. (1995), 'Chile con Chicago: A Review Essay', *Journal of Economic Literature*, vol. 33, pp. 1941-1949.

Bardhan, P. (1997), 'Corruption and Development: A Review of the Issues', *Journal of Economic Literature*, vol. 35, pp. 1320-1346.

Baron, J.N. and Hannan, M.T. (1994), 'The Impact of Economics on Contemporary Sociology', *Journal of Economic Literature*, vol. 32, pp. 1111-1146.

Barry, B. (1989), *Theories of Justice*, University of California Press, Berkeley.

Basu, K. (1984), 'The Right to Give Up Rights', *Economica*, vol. 51, pp. 413-422.

Becker, G.S. (1993), 'Nobel Lecture: The Economic Way of Looking at Behavior', *Journal of Political Economy*, vol. 101, pp. 385-409.

Bentsen, L. (Sen.) (1980), *Report on the January 1980 Economic Report of the President*, United States Government Printing Office, Washington, D.C.

Boland, L.A. (1981), 'On the Futility of Criticizing the Neoclassical Maximization Hypothesis', *American Economic Review*, vol. 71, pp. 1031-1036.

Bovard, J. (1995), *Lost Rights: The Destruction of American Liberty*, St. Martin's Griffin, New York.

Bowles, S. and Gintis, H. (1993), 'The Revenge of *homo economicus*: Contested Exchange and the Revival of Political Economy', *Journal of Economic Perspectives*, vol. 7, pp. 83-102.

Braguinsky, S. (1996), 'Corruption and Schumpeterian Growth in Different Economic Environments', *Contemporary Economic Policy*, vol. 14, pp. 14-25.

Buchanan, J.M. (1994a), 'Choosing What to Choose', *Journal of Institutional and Theoretical Economics*, vol. 150, pp. 123-135.

Buchanan, J.M. (1987), 'The Constitution of Economic Policy', *American Economic Review*, vol. 77, pp. 243-250.

Buchanan, J.M. (1991), *The Economics and the Ethics of Constitutional Order*, The University of Michigan Press, Ann Arbor.

Buchanan, J.M. (1994b), *Ethics and Economic Progress*, University of Oklahoma Press, Norman.

Buchanan, J.M. (1954a), 'Individual Choice in Voting and the Market', *Journal of Political Economy*, vol. 62, pp. 334-343.

Buchanan, J.M. (1986), *Liberty, Market and State: Political Economy in the 1980s*, New York University Press, New York.

Buchanan, J.M. (1954b), 'Social Choice, Democracy, and Free Markets', *Journal of Political Economy*, vol. 62, pp. 114-123.

Buchanan, J.M. and Wagner, R.E. (1977), *Democracy in Deficit: The Political Legacy of Lord Keynes*, Academic Press, New York.

Cheung, S.N.S. (1996), 'A Simplistic General Equilibrium Theory of Corruption', *Contemporary Economic Policy*, vol. 14, pp. 1-5.

Conlisk, J. (1996), 'Why Bounded Rationality?', *Journal of Economic Literature*, 34, pp. 669-700.

Council of Economic Advisers (1988), *Economic Report of the President*, United States Government Printing Office, Washington, D.C.

Cox, J.C. and Epstein, S. (1989), 'Preference Reversals without the Independence Axiom', *American Economic Review*, vol. 79, pp. 408-426.

Cullis, J.G. and Jones, P.R. (1998), "Towards a 'New' Outrageous Public Choice", *Journal of Socio-Economics*, vol. 27, pp. 623-640.

Davis, N.A. (1993), 'Contemporary deontology', in P. Singer (ed), *A Companion to Ethics*, Blackwell Publishers, Ltd, Cambridge, MA, pp. 205-218.

Deb, R., Pattanaik, P.K. and Razzolini, L. (1997), 'Game Forms, Rights, and the Efficiency of Social Outcomes', *Journal of Economic Theory*, vol. 72, pp. 74-95.

Demsetz, H. (1997), 'The Primacy of Economics: An Explanation of the Comparative Success of Economics in the Social Sciences', *Economic Inquiry*, vol. 35, pp. 1-11.

Dowell, R.S., Goldfarb, R.S., and Griffith, W.B. (1998), 'Economic Man As a Moral Individual', *Economic Inquiry*, vol. 36, pp. 645-653.

Duffie, D. and Sonnenschein, H. (1989), 'Arrow and General Equilibrium Theory', *Journal of Economic Literature*, vol. 27, pp. 565-598.

Dworkin, R. (1995), 'Rights as Trumps', in Waldron (1995).

Dworkin, R. (1978), *Taking Rights Seriously*, Harvard University Press, Cambridge.

Egide, M. and Marris, R. (eds) (1992), *Economics, Bounded Rationality and the Cognitive Revolution*, Edward Elgar, Aldershot, UK.

Elster, J. (1989), 'Social Norms and Economic Theory', *Journal of Economic Perspectives*, vol. 3, pp. 99-117.

Florence, R.E. (1999), 'An Analysis of PAC Contributions and Legislator Quality', *Atlantic Economic Journal*, vol. 27, pp. 59-73.

Frank, R.H. (1996), "The Political Economy of Preference Falsification: Timur Kuran's 'Private Truths, Public Lies'", *Journal of Economic Literature*, vol. 34, pp. 115-123.

Friedman, M. (1962), *Capitalism and Freedom*, University of Chicago Press, Chicago.

Furubotn, E.G. (1971), 'Economic Organization and Welfare Distribution', *The Swedish Journal of Economics*, vol. 73, pp. 409-416.

Furubotn, E.G. (1994), *Future Development of the New Institutional Economics: Extension of the Neoclassical Model or New Construct?*, Max-Planck Institute for Research into Economic Systems, Jena.

Furubotn, E.G. (1991). 'General Equilibrium Models, Transaction Costs, and the Concept of Efficient Allocation in a Capitalist Economy', *Journal of Institutional and Theoretical Economics*, vol. 147, pp. 662-686.

Furubotn, E.G. (1964), 'Investment Alternatives and the Supply Schedule of the Firm', *Southern Economic Journal*, vol. 31, pp. 21-37.

Furubotn, E.G. (1970), 'Long-Run Analysis and the Form of the Production Function', *Economia Internazionale*, vol. 23, pp. 3-35.

Furubotn, E.G. (1967), 'Observed Consumption Patterns and the Utility Tree', *Metroeconomica*, vol. 19, pp. 42-61.

Furubotn, E.G. (1965), 'The Orthodox Production Function and the Adaptability of Capital', *Western Economic Journal*, vol. 3, pp. 288-300.

Furubotn, E.G. (1997), 'Technological Choices and the Neoclassical Theory of Production', mimeo.

Furubotn, E.G. and Pejovich, S. (1974), *The Economics of Property Rights*, Ballinger, Cambridge, MA.

Furubotn, E.G. and Pejovich, S. (1972), 'Property Rights and Economic Theory: A Survey of the Recent Literature', *Journal of Economic Literature*, vol. 10, pp. 1137-1162.

Furubotn, E.G. and Richter, R. (1997), *Institutions and Economic Theory: The Contribution of the New Institutional Economics*, The University of Michigan Press, Ann Arbor.

Furubotn, E.G. and Richter, R. (1991), *The New Institutional Economics*, J.C.B. Mohr, Tübingen.

Gaertner, W., Pattanaik, P.K. and Suzumura, K. (1992), 'Individual Rights Revisited', *Economica*, vol. 59, pp. 161-178.

Gauthier , D. (1986), *Morals by Agreement*, Oxford University Press, Oxford.

Gibbard, A. (1974), 'A Pareto-Consistent Libertarian Claim', *Journal of Economic Theory*, vol. 7, pp. 388-410.

Goodin, R.E. (1993), 'Utility and the Good', in P. Singer (ed), *A Companion to Ethics*, Blackwell Publishers, Ltd, Cambridge, MA, pp. 241-248.

Gort, M. and Boddy, R. (1965), 'Vintage Effects and the Time Path of Investment in Production Relations', mimeographed, Conference on Research in Income and Wealth, National Bureau of Economic Research, New York.

Graaff, J.deV. (1967), *Theoretical Welfare Economics*, Cambridge University Press, Cambridge.

Haavelmo, T. (1997), 'Econometrics and the Welfare State', *American Economic Review*, vol. 87, pp. 13-15.

Hahn, R.W. (1998), 'Government Analysis of the Benefits and Costs of Regulation', *Journal of Economic Perspectives*, vol. 12, pp. 201-210.

Hatch, O. (Sen.) (1981), *Report to Accompany Senate Joint Resolution 58, Balanced Budget-Tax Limitation Amendment*, United States Government Printing Office, Washington, D.C.

Hausman, D.M. and McPherson, M.S. (1996), *Economic Analysis and Moral Philosophy*, Cambridge University Press, Cambridge.

Hausman, D.M. and McPherson, M.S. (1993), 'Taking Ethics Seriously: Economics and Contemporary Moral Philosophy', *Journal of Economic Literature*, vol. 31, pp. 671-731.

Hayek, F. (1960), *The Constitution of Liberty*, University of Chicago Press, Chicago.

Heiner, R.A. (1983), 'The Origin of Predictable Behavior', *American Economic Review*, vol. 73, pp. 560-595.

Hohfeld, W.N. (1919), *Fundamental Legal Conceptions as Applied in Judicial Reasoning*, Yale University Press, New Haven.

Jones, E.L. (1995), 'Culture and Its Relationship to Economic Change', *Journal of Institutional and Theoretical Economics*, vol. 151, pp. 269-285.

Keita, L.D. (1992), *Science, Rationality, and Neoclassical Economics*, University of Delaware Press, Newark.

Klamer, A. (1989), 'A Conversation with Amartya Sen', *Journal of Economic Perspectives*, vol. 3, pp. 135-150.

Kroszner, R.S. and Stratmann, T. (1998), 'Interest-Group Competition and the Organization of Congress: Theory and Evidence from Financial Services' Political Action Committees', *American Economic Review*, vol. 88, pp. 1163-1187.

Kymlicka, W. (1993), 'The Social Contract Tradition', in P. Singer (ed), *A Companion to Ethics*, Blackwell Publishers, Ltd, Cambridge, MA, pp. 186-196.

Lewin, S.B. (1996), 'Economics and Psychology: Lessons for Our Own Day from the Early Twentieth Century', *Journal of Economic Literature*, vol. 34, pp. 1293-1323.

Lui, F.T. (1996), 'Thru Aspects of Corruption', *Contemporary Economic Policy*, vol. 14, pp. 26-29.

Lyons, D. (1982), 'Utility and Rights', in J.R. Pennock and J.W. Chapman (eds), *Ethics, Economics and the Law: Nomos XXIV*, New York University Press, New York; reprinted in Waldron (1995).

McCloskey, D.M. (1983), 'The Rhetoric of Economics', *Journal of Economic Literature*, vol. 21, pp. 481-517.

Melitz, J. (1965), 'Friedman and Machlup on the Significance of Testing Economic Assumptions', *Journal of Political Economy*, vol. 73, pp. 37-60.

Miller, G.J. (1997), 'The Impact of Economics on Contemporary Political Science', *Journal of Economic Literature*, vol. 35, pp. 1173-1204.

Miller, M.S. (1983), 'Methodology and the Theory of Consumer Behavior', *Review of Social Economy*, vol. 41, pp. 39-51.

Moore, M.O. (1992), 'Rules or Politics?: An Empirical Analysis of ITC Anti-Dumping Decisions', *Economic Inquiry*, vol. 30, pp. 449-466.

Muller, J.Z. (1993), *Adam Smith in His Time and Ours*, Princeton University Press, Princeton.

Murrell, P. (1995), 'The Transition According to Cambridge, Mass.', *Journal of Economic Literature*, vol. 33, pp. 164-178.

Nee, V.(1998), 'Norms and Networks in Economic and Organizational Performance', *American Economic Association Papers and Proceedings*, vol. 88, pp. 85-89.

Nelson, J.A. (1995), 'Feminism and Economics', *Journal of Economic Perspectives*, vol. 9, pp. 131-148.

North, D.C. (1994), 'Economic Performance Through Time', *American Economic Review*, vol. 84, pp. 359-368.

Novshek, W. and Sonnenschein, H. (1987), 'General Equilibrium with Free Entry: A Synthetic Approach to the Theory of Perfect Competition', *Journal of Economic Literature*, vol. 25, pp. 1281-1306.

Nozick, R. (1974), *Anarchy, State and Utopia*, Basic Books, Inc., Publishers, New York.

Office of Management and Budget (1999), *Budget of the United States Government, Fiscal Year 2000*, United States Government Printing Office, Washington, D.C.

O'Neill, O. (1993), 'Kantian Ethics', in P. Singer (ed), *A Companion to Ethics*, Blackwell Publishers, Ltd, Cambridge, MA, pp. 175-185.

Pareto, V. (1896), 'Cours d' Economie Politique', cited in Hatch (1981).

Persky, J. (1995), 'Retrospective: The ethology of *homo economicus'*, *Journal of Economic Perspectives*, vol. 9, pp. 221-231.

Pettit, P. (1993), 'Consequentialism', in P. Singer (ed), *A Companion to Ethics*, Blackwell Publishers, Ltd, Cambridge, MA, pp. 230-240.

Pingle, M. (1992), 'Costly Optimization: An Experiment', *Journal of Economic Behavior and Organization*, vol. 17, pp. 3-30.

Pollak, R.A. (1985), 'A Transaction Cost Approach to Families and Households', *Journal of Economic Literature*, vol. 13, pp. 581-608.

Prybyla, J.S. (1993), 'The Interplay of Economics and Politics in the Transformation of Social Systems', *Vital Speeches of the Day*, vol. 59, pp. 603-608.

Prybyla, J.S. (1995), 'Modernization and Modernity in the Process of Economic Growth', *Issues and Studies*, vol. 31, pp. 1-27.

Rawls, J. (1971), *A Theory of Justice*, The Belknap Press of Harvard University, Cambridge.

Riley, J. (1989), 'Rights to Liberty in Purely Private Matters, Part I', *Economic Philosophy*, vol. 5, pp. 121-166.

Robinson, J. (1962), *Economic Philosophy*, C.A. Watts & Co., London.

Roth, T.P. (1973), 'Classical vs. Process Analysis and the Form of the Production Function', *The Engineering Economist*, vol. 19, pp. 47-54.

Roth, T.P. (1974), 'The Demand for a Single Variable Productive Service and the Adaptability of Capital', *Artha Vijnana*, vol. 15, pp. 421-431.

Roth, T.P. (1979), 'Empirical Cost Curves and the Production-Theoretic Short-Run: A Reconciliation', *Quarterly Review of Economics and Business*, vol. 19, pp. 35-47.

Roth, T.P. (1977), 'Imperfect Knowledge and the Problem of Choice Among Alternative Production Techniques', *The Engineering Economist*, vol. 22, pp. 277-297.

Roth, T.P. (1994), *Information, Ideology and Freedom: The Disenfranchised Electorate*, University Press of America, Lanham, MD, New York and London.

Roth, T.P. (1975), 'The Multi-Equation Utility Function, Information, and the Optimal Commodity Bundle', *Metroeconomica*, vol. 27, pp. 137-149.

Roth, T.P. (1998), *The Present State of Consumer Theory: The Implications for Social Welfare Theory*, University Press of America, Lanham, MD, New York, Oxford.

Roth, T.P. (1972), 'The Subjective Production Function: An Approach to Its Determination', *The Engineering Economist*, vol. 17, pp. 249-259.

Rothschild, K.W. (1993), *Ethics and Economic Theory*, Edward Elgar, Aldershot, UK.

Sandmo, A. (1990), 'Buchanan on Political Economy: A Review Article', *Journal of Economic Literature*, vol. 28, pp. 50-65.

Scruton, R. (1994), *Modern Philosophy: An Introduction and Survey*, Penguin Books, New York.

Sen, A. (1986), 'Foundations of Social Choice Theory: An Epilogue', in J. Elster and A. Hylland (eds), *Foundations of Social Choice Theory*, Cambridge University Press, Cambridge, pp. 213-248.

Sen, A. (1970), 'The Impossibility of a Paretian Liberal', *Journal of Political Economy*, vol. 78, pp. 152-157.

Sen, A. (1992), *Inequality Reexamined*, Harvard University Press, Cambridge.

Sen, A. (1983), 'Liberty and Social Choice', *Journal of Philosophy*, vol. 80, pp. 5-28.

Sen, A. (1976), 'Liberty, Unanimity and Rights', *Economica*, vol. 43, pp. 217-245.

Sen, A. (1995), 'Rationality and Social Choice', *American Economic Review*, vol. 85, pp. 1-24.

Simon, H.A. (1955), 'A Behavioral Model of Rational Choice', *Quarterly Journal of Economics*, vol. 69, pp. 99-118.

Simon, H.A. (1978), 'Rationality as Process and as Product of Thought', *American Economic Association Papers and Proceedings*, vol. 68, pp. 1-16.

Simon, H.A. (1966), 'Theories of Decision-Making in Economics and Behavioural Science', in *Surveys of Economic Theory*, Vol. III, Macmillan, London, pp. 1-28.

Smith, A. (1759), *The Theory of Moral Sentiments*, A. Kincaid and J. Bell, Edinburgh.

Smith, V.L. (1994), 'Economics in the Laboratory', *Journal of Economic Perspectives*, vol. 8, pp. 113-131.

Staff (January 6, 1995), 'For the Record: New House Rules', *The New York Times*, p. A10.

Stigler, G. (1987), *The Theory of Price*, Macmillan Publishing Company, New York.

Stiglitz, J. (1998), 'The Private Uses of Public Interests: Incentives and Information', *Journal of Economic Perspectives*, vol. 12, pp. 3-22.

Stiglitz, J. (1994), *Whither Socialism*, MIT Press. Cambridge.

Sugden, R. (1993), 'Welfare, Resources, and Capabilities: A Review of *Inequality Reexamined* by Amartya Sen', *Journal of Economic Literature*, vol. 31, pp. 1947-1962.

Temple, J. (1999), 'The New Growth Evidence', *Journal of Economic Literature*, vol. 37, pp. 112-156.

Tullock, G. (1996), 'Corruption Theory and Practice', *Contemporary Economic Policy*, vol. 14, pp. 6-13.

Tversky, A. and Thaler, R.H. (1990), 'Preference Reversals', *Journal of Economic Perspectives*, vol. 4, pp. 201-211.

Waldron, J. (ed) (1995), *Theories of Rights*, Oxford University Press, Oxford.

Wilde, K.D., LeBaron, A.D. and Israelsen, D. (1985), 'Knowledge, Uncertainty and Behavior', *American Economic Association Papers and Proceedings*, vol. 75, pp. 403-408.

Williamson, O.E. (1994), 'Concluding Comment', *Journal of Institutional and Theoretical Economics*, vol. 150, pp. 320-324.

Williamson, O.E. (1993), 'Contested Exchange versus the Governance of Contractual Relations', *Journal of Economic Perspectives*, vol. 7, pp. 103-108.

Williamson, O.E. (1985), *The Economic Institutions of Capitalism*, The Free Press, New York.

Wong, S. (1973), "The 'F-Twist' and the Methodology of Paul Samuelson", *American Economic Review*, vol. 63, pp. 312-325.

Index